YOUNG PEOPLE'S STORY OF
OUR HERITAGE

YOUNG PEOPLE'S
STORY OF
OUR HERITAGE

THE ANCIENT WORLD

by

V. M. HILLYER and E. G. HUEY

New Edition Designed and Revised by Childrens Press, Chicago

Consultants

William T. Nichol, Principal
Charles Gates Dawes Elementary School, Evanston, Illinois

John R. Lee, Professor of Education
Northwestern University, Evanston, Illinois

Meredith Press, New York

Illustrations in the order in which they appear

Library of Congress Catalog Card Number: 66-11329

Contents

Acknowledgments

Cover painting: Attila and his Huns preparing to attack
John Hollis—Hollis Associates

Page 2: Statue of Alexander the Great on his Horse, Bucephalus. Museo Nazionale, Naples.
Alinari-Art Reference Bureau

Frontis: A 4th-century Persian metal dish
Courtesy of the Smithsonian Institution, Freer Gallery of Art, Washington, D.C.

Opposite: Model of a Roman merchant ship, 50 A.D., built by August F. Crabtree
Courtesy, The Mariners Museum, Newport News, Virginia

Designer: John Hollis

Project Editor: Joan Downing

Editorial Staff: Frances Dyra,
Mary Reidy, Geri Stoller

THE ANCIENT WORLD

500 B.C.—500 A.D.

North Sea
Baltic Sea
BRITAIN
GAUL
Alps
Pyrenees
SPAIN
CORSICA
ITALY
Rome
Adriatic Sea
SARDINIA
Caspian Sea
Black Sea
THRACE
Byzantium
MACEDONIA
Aegean Sea
GREECE
Athens
ASIA MINOR
Nineveh
Tigris River
Euphrates River
SICILY
Carthage
Sparta
AFRICA
Mediterranean Sea
CRETE
CYPRUS
Babylon
MESOPOTAMIA
Persian Gulf
CYRENAICA
Alexandria
EGYPT
ARABIA
Nile River
Red Sea

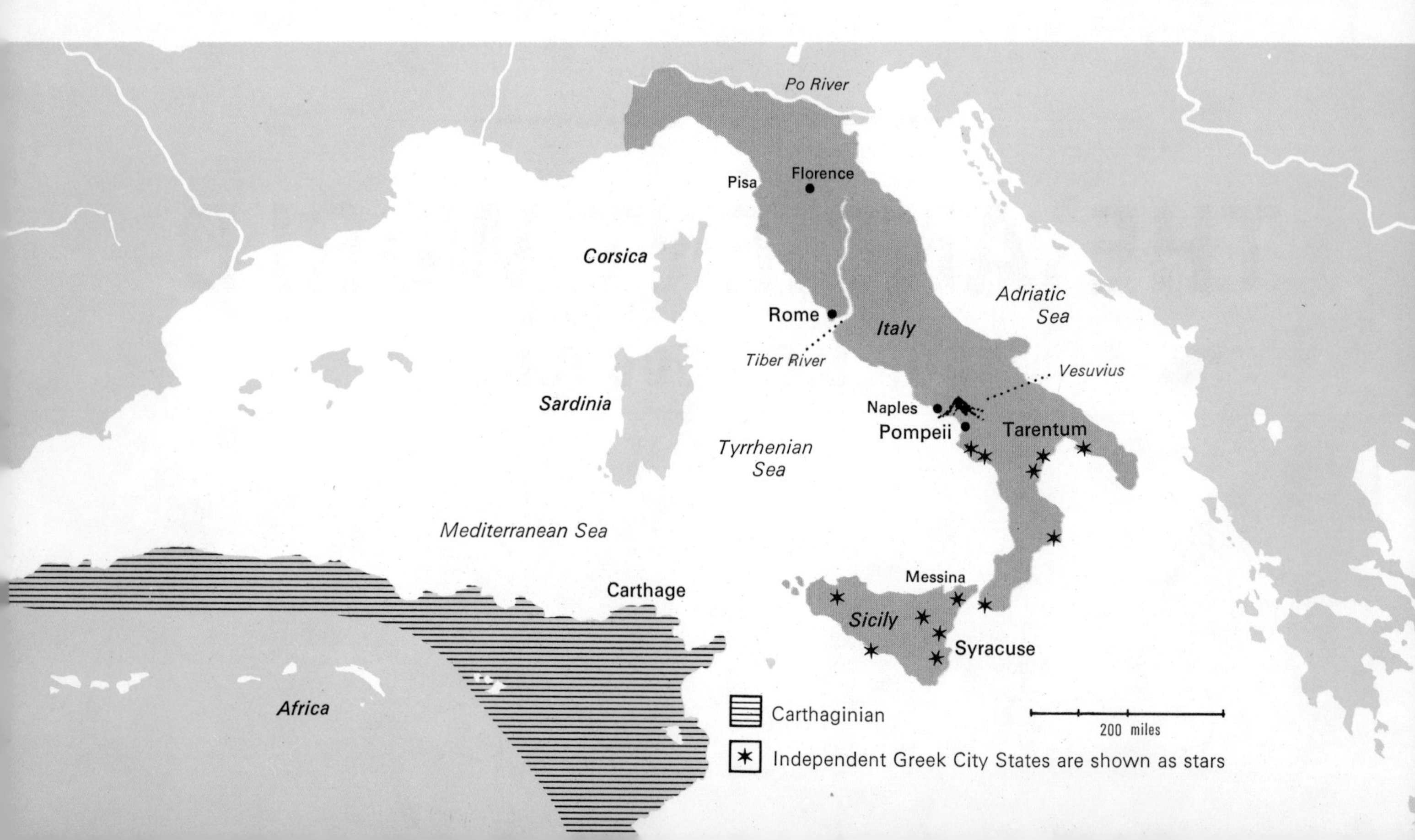
Po River
Pisa
Florence
Corsica
Adriatic Sea
Rome
Italy
Tiber River
Vesuvius
Sardinia
Naples
Pompeii
Tarentum
Tyrrhenian Sea
Mediterranean Sea
Messina
Carthage
Sicily
Syracuse
Africa
Carthaginian
200 miles
Independent Greek City States are shown as stars

The Roman Republic

In the sixth century B.C. there were two classes of people in Rome, just as there were in Athens. The wealthy people were called *patricians* (pah-trish′ans), and the poor people were called *plebeians* (pleh-bee′ yans), or *plebs*. We use the same words now and often call people who are rich and aristocratic, "patricians," and people who are poor and uneducated, "plebeians." The patricians were allowed to vote and were full-fledged citizens. For a long time the plebeians were not allowed to vote, even though they were protected by Rome; but eventually they were given the right to vote.

In 509 B.C. Rome had a king named Tarquin (tar′ qwin) who decided that the plebeians should not be allowed to vote. Tarquin also tried to limit the vote of the patricians. The plebeians would not stand for this, and together with the patricians, they drove King Tarquin out of the city.

After King Tarquin had been driven out of Rome, the Romans started what is called a *republic*. Republic comes from a Latin word and means public affair. This new government was a public affair, but at first only the patricians were allowed to run it. To the Romans at this time, the republic really meant the absence of a king or emperor. It also meant that only some of the people elected the leaders. The Romans did not want only one man to rule. They were afraid he might make himself king, and they did not want to have another king. Tarquin was the last king Rome ever had.

The new Roman republic had a senate made up of patricians. Two of these patrician senators were elected by the senate to rule Rome. These rulers were called consuls and could serve for one year only. They were the commanders of the army, as well as the rulers of Rome.

John Hollis—Hollis Associates

opposite above: The Mediterranean World

opposite below: Detail of large map showing Italy

Bob Brunton—Hollis Associates

Each consul had a bodyguard of twelve men who were called *lictors* (lick'turz). Each lictor carried an ax tied up in a bundle of sticks. This bundle of sticks with the ax head sticking out in the middle or at the end was known as the *fasces* (fass'eez). The fasces was a symbol of the ruler's power. It meant that the consuls had power to punish by whipping with the sticks or by chopping off one's head with the ax. Some modern coins and postage stamps have fasces pictured on them. Perhaps you have seen fasces used as ornaments or decoration around monuments or public buildings.

As you can see, the patricians were the ruling class. They were allowed to vote and owned most of the property. Only patricians served in the senate, which made laws and elected consuls and judges. The plebeians were not allowed to vote or to hold office, and so had very little to say about the government. Nor were they allowed to marry patricians. But they *were* expected to pay taxes and fight in the Roman wars. Because the Romans were fighting nearly all the time, the plebeians often had to leave their farms to go off to war, even though their harvest and farms might be ruined by the time they returned. And if they owed money they couldn't pay, they lost their land and sometimes were sold into slavery.

The plebeians tried many ways to gain more power—once they even moved away and started their own town! Finally, because the patricians needed the plebs—to fight the wars and pay taxes—they gave the plebs some rights. In about 494 B.C. plebeians were given the right to elect their own officials, called *tribunes*. These men were supposed to protect the plebeians from unjust laws that might be made by the senate. The tribunes protected plebeians by the *veto*. Veto is a Latin word that means "I forbid." The tribunes could *forbid* the senate to pass laws that were not fair to the plebeians. Even so, plebs had trouble with the patrician senate. The trouble came mainly because the laws of Rome had never been written down. Finally in 450 B.C., the plebeians demanded that the laws be written. As a result, the laws were carved on tablets of bronze and posted in the Forum for all to see. They were called the *Twelve Tables*.

By 445 B.C., the plebs gained the right to marry patricians; and eventually they were allowed to hold certain elective offices. At last it was decided that one of the two

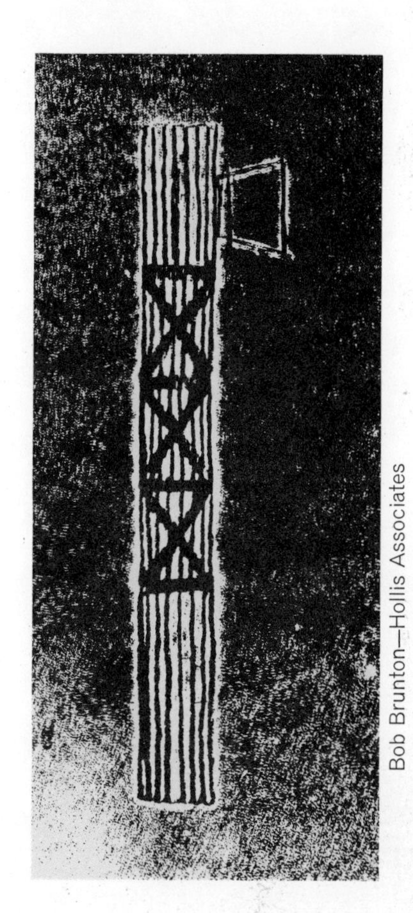

Bob Brunton—Hollis Associates

above: The fasces carried by the Roman lictors

opposite above: Typical Roman dress in the 6th century B.C. Left: the peasant class, or plebeians; center: the middle class; right: the aristocratic class, or patricians.

opposite below: A relief showing a scene in the Roman senate. Palazzo Sacchetti, Rome.

Alinari-Art Reference Bureau

right: A typical Roman marketplace showing Romans of all classes milling about. Merchants covered their wares with canopies to protect them from the weather.

opposite: Cincinnatus being asked to leave his plow to become dictator

consuls would be a plebeian. When the plebeians were granted full citizenship they created a new nobility—based on money. The plebeians who were elected to public office were very wealthy. Anyone who was poor could not afford to hold office, and the wealthy plebeians often acted to protect their wealth rather than to represent the poor.

The gradual development of democracy in Rome took about 200 years. This Roman democracy is meaningful to us even now, for many governmental systems and laws that are in effect in a great part of the world today began in Rome—more than two thousand years ago!

In 458 B.C. the Romans almost lost some of the gains they had made in democracy. A man named Cincinnatus,

who had a farm on the Tiber River, was very wise and good and the people of Rome honored and trusted him. One day when an enemy was about to attack the city—in those days there always seemed to be enemies ready to attack Rome on any excuse—the people needed a leader and a general. They thought of Cincinnatus and asked him to be *dictator*.

Dictator was the name Romans gave to a man called upon to command the army and rule the people in time of great danger. A dictator was allowed to rule for only six months. During this time he could act alone—without the help of the senators or tribunes. Cincinnatus agreed to become dictator and left his plow. He went with the people to the city, got together an army, went out and defeated the enemy, and returned to Rome—and he did all this within twenty-four hours!

The people were so pleased with the way in which Cincinnatus had saved Rome that they wanted him to keep right on being their leader in time of peace. Even though they hated kings, they wanted to make him their king! But Cincinnatus did not want any such thing. His duty done, he wanted to return to his wife and his humble farm home. So in spite of what many would have thought was a wonderful chance, he did go back to his plow; he chose to be just a simple farmer instead of king of Rome. His decision not to become king saved the democracy that Rome had worked so hard to establish.

Greece vs. Persia: Darius at the Plain of Marathon

Do you know what the two little letters *vs.* mean when they are placed between words? These letters stand for the Latin word *versus*, which means "against."

There was to be a great match between Greece and Persia, but it wasn't a game. It was a fight for life—the very small country of Greece against the huge empire of Persia, or Greece *vs.* Persia.

Cyrus (sye′russ), a great Persian king, had conquered Babylon and many other countries. In fact he had kept on conquering countries until Persia ruled most of the world—all except Greece and Rome.

In about 500 B.C. this vast Persian Empire had a new ruler named Darius (deh-ree′us). He was called "Great King." When Darius looked at a map and realized that he ruled most of the world, it seemed a pity to him that there should be a little country like Greece that was not his!

Darius decided that he must have this land called Greece to complete his empire. Besides, the Greeks had given him some trouble. They had helped some of his Greek subjects in Asia Minor to rebel against him. Darius said, "I must punish these Greeks for what they have done and then add their country to mine." So in 492 B.C. he told his son-in-law, Mardonius (mar-doe′nee-us), to go over to Greece and conquer it.

Mardonius started out with a fleet of ships and an army of men to do the punishing. The fleet was collected from all the cities in Asia Minor that had already been conquered and were under the rule of Darius. So besides Persians, there were also Phoenicians, Egyptians, and even some Greeks in the army Mardonius collected!

But before the fleet could even reach Greece, a storm struck near Mount Athos and wrecked the ships. The Persians had to go back home without even seeing a Greek face, much less conquering the country!

Darius was very angry at this, angry with his son-in-law and angry with the gods who, he thought, had wrecked his ships. He made up his mind that he himself would do the punishing and conquering the next time.

opposite top: The Persian Empire. Note its size as compared with that of Greece.

---

opposite bottom: Greece in the 6th century B.C.

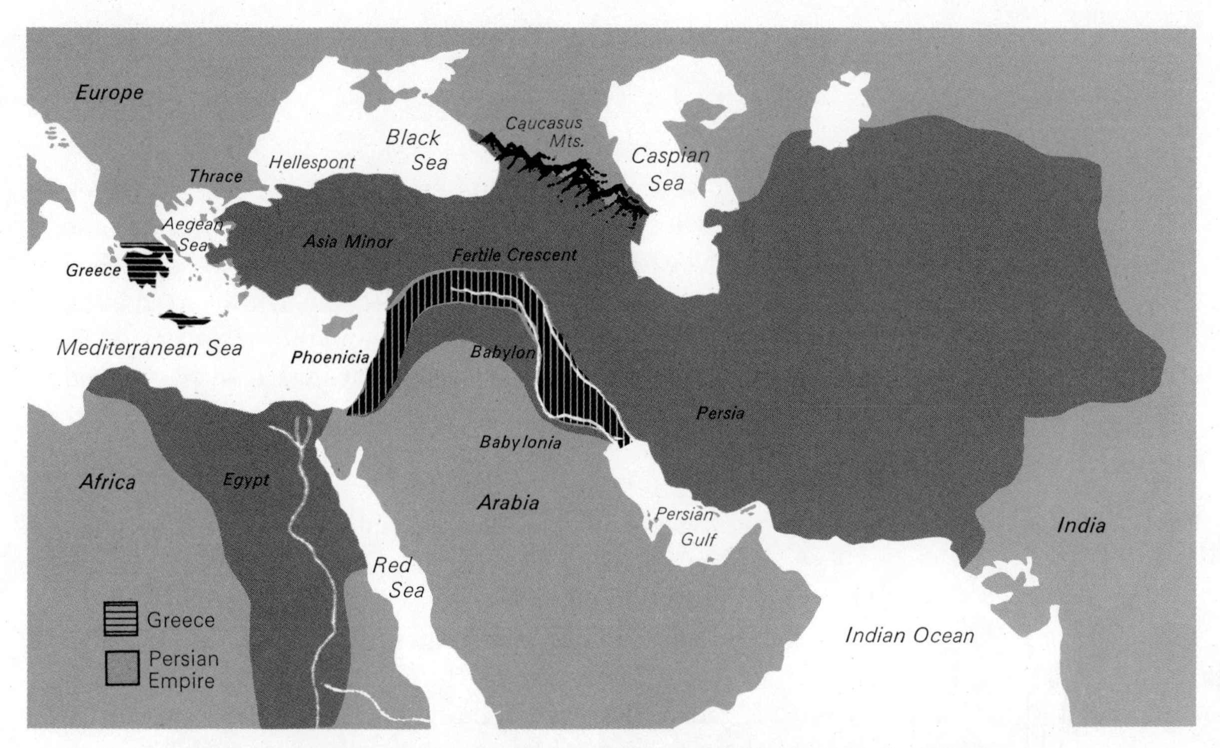
Europe
Black Sea
Caucasus Mts.
Caspian Sea
Thrace
Hellespont
Aegean Sea
Asia Minor
Greece
Fertile Crescent
Mediterranean Sea
Phoenicia
Babylon
Persia
Babylonia
Africa
Egypt
Arabia
Persian Gulf
India
Red Sea
Indian Ocean
Greece
Persian Empire

Macedonia
Thrace
Samothrace
Hellespont
Mt. Athos
Thessaly
Land of Troy
Aegean Sea
Asia Minor
Ionian Sea
Thermopylae Pass
Marathon
Delphi
Salamis
Athens
Peloponnesus
Delos
Siphnos
Sparta
Mediterranean Sea
Rhodes
The route of Darius
The route of Mardonius
The route of Xerxes
Crete

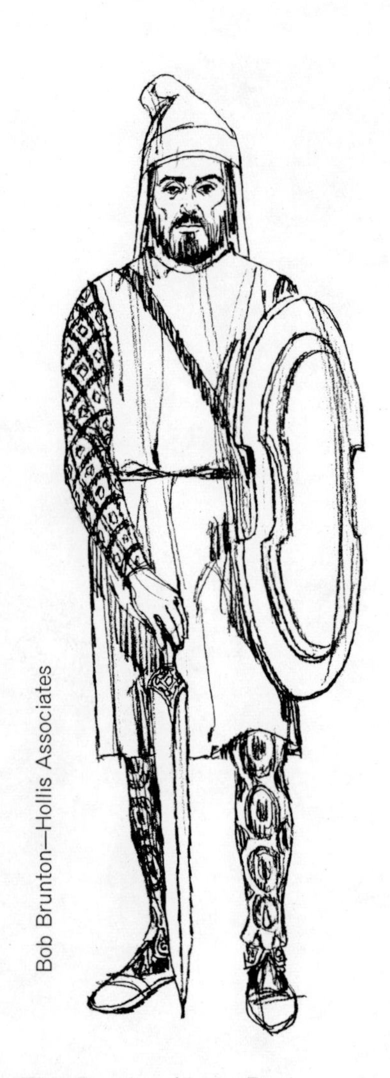
Bob Brunton—Hollis Associates

The Persian king, Darius

First, however, he sent his messengers to all the Greek cities and ordered them to give him their land and become his subjects peaceably, without a fight. If they agreed, they were to send him some earth and some water as a sign that he was their king and ruled over land and sea.

The people in most of the Greek cities were so frightened by the threat of Darius and by his mighty power that they gave in at once. They sent earth and water as they were told to do.

But the people in Athens and Sparta were not afraid. They refused to send the earth and water, even though they held only two small cities.

Athens took Darius' messenger and threw him into a well, saying, "There is earth and water for you, help yourself," and Sparta did likewise. Then these two cities joined their forces. They called on all their neighbors to help them in a fight for their independence against Darius and Persia.

So Darius made ready to conquer first Athens and then Sparta.

In order to reach Athens his army had to be carried across the Aegean Sea in boats. Of course, in those days there were no steamships. Steamships were invented thousands of years later. The only way to make a boat go was to use sails or oars. To make a large boat move with oars, it was necessary to have many, many rowers. They sat in three rows, one above the other, on both sides of the boat.

A boat with three rows of rowers on each side was called a *trireme* (try'reem). Darius needed about 500 of these boats to carry his army over the sea to Greece. Each of these 500 boats carried, besides the rowers or crew, about 200 soldiers and the food, water, and other supplies they needed.

The Persians set sail across the sea in 490 B.C. This time there was no storm, and they reached the shore of Greece at the Bay of Marathon safely. They marched to the plain of Marathon, which was about twenty-six miles from Athens.

When the Athenians heard that the Persians were coming, they wanted the Spartans to come in a hurry to help, as they had promised to do. There were no telegraphs or telephones or railroads in those days, of course, so there was no way in which the Athenians could send a message to the Spartans except to have it carried by hand.

So they called on a famous runner named Pheidippides (fie-dip′ih-deez) to carry the message. Pheidippides ran the whole way from Athens to Sparta—about one hundred and fifty miles! He ran night and day, hardly stopping to rest or to eat, and on the second day he was in Sparta with the message.

The Spartans, however, sent back word that they couldn't start immediately, for they were having a religious festival; also the moon wasn't full, and they believed it would be unlucky to start when the moon wasn't full. They said they would come when the moon was full.

But the Athenians couldn't wait for the moon. They knew the Persians would be in Athens before then, and certainly didn't want the Persians to get that close!

So all the fighting men in Athens left their city and marched twenty-six miles to meet the Persians on the plain of Marathon.

Nine thousand Athenians were led by a general named Miltiades (mill-tee′uh-deez). One thousand more men from a little nearby town called Plataea (plah-tee′uh) joined the Athenians. Plataea was friendly with Athens and wished to help her. So there were ten thousand soldiers in all. The Greek writers say that there may have been ten times as many Persians as there were Greeks. If that is true, there were ten Persian soldiers to every one Greek soldier. But we are fairly sure that the writers exaggerated. Also, the Persians had divided their army. They had left some men on the triremes, and so probably there were only about twenty-five thousand Persians at the plain of Marathon. Twenty-five thousand Persians and only ten thousand Greeks! It didn't seem that the Greeks had a chance of winning.

Persian soldiers

The Greeks, however, were trained athletes, and their whole manner of life kept them in excellent physical condition. The Persians were no match for them, and that very small band of Greeks beat the very large Persian army with no trouble at all!

Records say that Persia lost six thousand soldiers and that Greece lost fewer than two hundred! Of course, the Greeks' wonderful general, Miltiades, had made a surprise attack on the Persian camp. Also, the Greeks used spears, which were good at close range, while the Persians used bows and arrows, which were good only at a distance. But even more important than this was the fact that the Greeks were fighting to save their homes and their families. They *had* to win—and they did!

Perhaps you have heard the fable of the hound who chased the hare. The hare—surprisingly—escaped. When the hound was laughed at for not catching the little hare he said, "I was only running for my supper; the hare was running for his life." The Persian soldiers were not fighting for their homes or families, for they were on the other side of the sea. It made little difference to them who won anyway, for they were only hirelings or slaves. They were fighting for a king, because he ordered them to do so.

Naturally the Greeks were overjoyed by this victory. Pheidippides, the famous runner, who had returned to Marathon, started at once to carry the happy news back to Athens. He ran the whole distance without stopping. But he had not had time to rest up from his long run to Sparta, which he had taken only a few days before. He ran so fast that as soon as he had reached Athens and gasped the news to the Athenians in the marketplace he dropped dead!

In honor of this famous run, we have a Marathon race in the Olympic Games in which the athletes run the same distance Pheidippides ran—twenty-six miles.

As we mentioned, this battle of Marathon took place in 490 B.C. It is one of the most famous battles in all history, for the great Persian army was beaten by one little city and its neighbor. The Persians had to go back to their homes in disgrace.

A little handful of people who governed themselves had defeated a great king with a large army of soldiers.

But this was not the last the Greeks were to see of the Persians.

Historical Pictures Service, Chicago

Flight of the Persians after the Battle of Marathon

Greece vs. Persia: Xerxes Crosses the Hellespont

Alinari-Art Reference Bureau

Portrait bust of Aristides. Museo Capitolino, Rome.

Darius was angrier than ever after his defeat at Marathon, and was still more determined to whip those stubborn Greeks. He began to get ready for one more invasion attempt. This time, however, Darius made up his mind that he would gather such a big army and navy that the Greeks would have absolutely no chance against it. And he made a solemn oath to destroy the Greeks. For several years he gathered troops and supplies and planned his great victory; but after all this preparation, before he could carry out his wonderful, foolproof plan, he died!

But Darius had a son named Xerxes (zurk′ seez) who was just as determined as his father had been that the Greeks must be beaten. So Xerxes continued his father's preparations and went right on getting the army ready for war with the Greeks.

The Greeks were just as sure that they must *not* be beaten, so they, too, went on getting ready for the invasion of the Persians! They knew that sooner or later the Persians would come back and try again.

Now at this time in Athens there were two important men who both wanted to be the one chosen to lead the Athenians. One was named Aristides (air-iss-tie′deez), and the other was Themistocles (theh-miss′tuh-kleez).

Themistocles urged the Athenians to get ready for what he knew was coming—the next war with Persia. Especially he urged the Athenians to build a fleet of boats, for they had *no* boats at this time and the Persians had many.

Aristides, who was called "Aristides the Just" because he was so wise and fair, didn't believe in Themistocles' scheme. He thought it would be a foolish expense to build boats, and he tried to talk the people out of building them.

Some of the Athenians wanted to get rid of Aristides because they thought he was wrong and Themistocles was right. So they waited until the time came for the assembly to vote to *ostracize* (ahs′trah-size) anyone they didn't want around. If enough people voted against Aristides, he would be *ostracized*, or sent away from Athens for a long time—maybe for as long as ten years!

When the day for voting came, a man who could not write and did not know Aristides by sight happened to ask his help in voting. Aristides asked what name he should write, and the man replied, "Aristides." Aristides did not tell the man who he was, but only said: "Why do you want to get rid of this man? Has he done anything wrong?"

"Oh, no," the voter replied. "He hasn't done anything wrong;" but with a long sigh he said, "I'm so tired of hearing him always called 'The Just'!"

Aristides must have been surprised by this unreasonable answer, but nevertheless he wrote his own name for the voter. Six thousand people voted to ostracize Aristides, so he was sent away, or exiled.

Though it may not seem quite fair that this happened to Aristides, it was fortunate that Themistocles had his way. The Athenians began preparing for the coming war. They built a fleet of two hundred triremes and tried to convince all the cities in Greece to join the fight against Persia. They were partly successful, and other cities added one hundred and fifty triremes to the Athenians' two hundred. Sparta was famous as a city of soldiers and so was made the leader of all the others in case of war.

And then, in 480 B.C., just ten years after the battle of Marathon, the great Persian army attacked Greece. It had been brought together from all parts of the huge Persian Empire.

A history of the Persian and Greek wars was written by a Greek named Herodotus (heh-rahd′uh-tuss). For this reason Herodotus is called the "Father of History." Someday you may study ancient Greek and read what he wrote in his own language. Of course, at that time, there was very little history to write. Up to the time of Herodotus, men knew very little about things that had happened before—and even less had been written down!

Herodotus traveled to many places and talked to many people. His books describe the background of the wars and his long journeys to Egypt and other countries. In his books he wrote the tales that were told to him during his

Historical Pictures Service, Chicago

Ostraka, used in a vote of ostracism

Alinari-Art Reference Bureau

above: Portrait bust of Herodotus. Museo Nazionale, Naples.

opposite: Xerxes' pontoon bridge

travels. He wrote about the kings of Persia and how they conquered many different countries and built up a large empire. He also wrote about the Greek states and how they disagreed and how they became united for awhile to defend themselves against the Persians.

Herodotus tells us that in 480 B.C. there were over two million soldiers in the Persian army, but modern historians think that there were only two hundred thousand. This huge army came from an empire that included Indians, Assyrians, Caspians, Ethiopians, Persians, and Medes.

Two hundred thousand is not as large an army as two million, but it still is a large group of men. How could the Persians get so many soldiers over to Greece? Not all of them could be carried to Greece by boat. Even the largest triremes held only a few hundred men, and it would have taken many, many triremes to carry them. So Xerxes decided to have part of his army march around the Aegean Sea and into Greece. It would be a long march, but it was the only way.

There was a strip of water called a *strait*, something like a wide river, right across the path that the Persian army had to take. This strait was then called the Hellespont. It is still there, but if you look on the map now you will find it is now called the Dardanelles. There was no bridge across the Hellespont, for it was almost a mile wide, and there weren't any bridges as long as that in those days. So Xerxes fastened boats together in a line that stretched from one shore to the other shore. Over these boats he built a platform to make a bridge for his army to walk across! Many people after Xerxes used his idea for building bridges by floating them on the water. Many military bridges are still built this way. They are called *pontoon* bridges.

Hardly had Xerxes finished building the bridge, however, when a storm destroyed it. Xerxes was so angry that he ordered his men to whip the water of the Hellespont as if it were a slave he were punishing! Then he built another bridge. This time the water behaved itself, and his soldiers were able to cross safely.

Xerxes' fleet followed the army as closely as it could along the shore. The army came down through the north of Greece. The soldiers marched through Thrace, Macedonia, and Thessaly, overrunning everything in its way. It seemed that nothing on earth could stop the Persians.

Bob Brunton—Hollis Associates

Greece vs. Persia: Thermopylae Pass and the Bay of Salamis

To reach Athens the Persians had to go through a narrow passageway with mountains on one side and water on the other. This pass is called Thermopylae (thair-mop′uh-lee). You might guess what Thermopylae means if you notice that the first part of the word is like "thermos," which means "hot." A thermos bottle, as you know, keeps things hot. As a matter of fact, Thermopylae meant "hot gateway." It was named that because there were hot springs near this natural gateway to Greece.

The Greeks decided that the best place to stop the Persians would be at this pass. Here a few Greek soldiers could fight well against a much larger number.

They also decided to send to the pass the very best soldiers in Greece and the best general they had. The Spartan king, who was named Leonidas (lay-on'ih-dus)—which in Greek means "like a lion"—was the one chosen to be the Greek general at Thermopylae. He took seven thousand Greek soldiers to block the way of two hundred thousand Persians! Three hundred of the Greek soldiers were Spartans, who had been taught that they must never surrender, never give up. A Spartan mother would say to her son, "Come back with your shield or on it." That meant that the soldier should either win or die trying. It would have been a disgrace for him to come back alive from a battle that had been lost.

When Xerxes found his way blocked by this small band of soldiers, he sent messengers to order them to surrender. Leonidas replied, "Come and take us."

Since there was nothing left for Xerxes to do but fight, he started his army forward. For two days the Persians fought the Greeks, but Leonidas still held the pass, and the Persians were unable to get through.

Then a Greek traitor and coward, who thought he might save his own life and be given a rich prize, went to Xerxes. He told him of a secret path over the mountains by which he and his army might slip through and get around Leonidas and his soldiers who blocked the way.

The next morning Leonidas learned that the Persians had found out about this path and were already on the way through it. There was still a chance, however, for his men to escape. Leonidas told his troops that those who wanted to could leave. Most of the Greeks left. Those who remained knew that the fight was hopeless and that it meant certain death for all of them. But about one thousand men, including all the three hundred Spartans, stood by their leader, for, said they, "We have been ordered to hold the pass, and a Spartan obeys orders, and never surrenders, no matter what happens."

So there Leonidas and his men fought to the bitter end until every man was killed.

The gateway to the city of Athens was now open, and things looked very bad for the Greeks. There was nothing to prevent the Persians from marching over the dead

Alinari-Art Reference Bureau

above: Portrait bust of Leonidas. Villa Albani, Rome.

opposite: The Battle of Thermopylae Pass

opposite top: Ruins of the Temple of Delphi

opposite bottom: The Battle of the Bay of Salamis

bodies of Leonidas and his men and straight on to Athens.

The Athenians, wondering what was to happen to them, hurriedly went to the oracle at the town of Delphi (del'fye) and asked what they should do. The oracle was a person thought to have special powers of seeing into the future and knowing what should be done about keeping something terrible from happening.

The Delphic oracle replied that the city of Athens itself was doomed, that it would be destroyed, there was no hope for it, but that the Athenians themselves would be saved by wooden walls.

This answer sounded like a riddle—in fact the oracle's answers usually *did* sound like riddles—and the meaning seemed hard to figure out. Themistocles, however, said that he knew the answer. You remember that it was he who had been working so hard to have a fleet of ships built. Themistocles said that the oracle meant these ships when it spoke of the wooden walls.

So the Athenians, following what they thought was the advice of the oracle, left their city as Themistocles had told them to do. They boarded the ships, which were nearby in a bay called Salamis (sahl'uh-mus). The women, children, and other citizens who were not fighting were taken to the island of Salamis and the rest of the people remained on the ships that were anchored in the bay. The Persian army reached Athens and found it deserted. So they destroyed the town as the oracle had predicted they would. Then they marched on to the Bay of Salamis, where the Athenians' fleet lay at anchor. Here, on a hill overlooking the bay, Xerxes had a throne built for himself so that he could sit as if he were in a theater looking at a play and watch his own large fleet destroy the much smaller one of the Greeks.

The Greek fleet was commanded by Themistocles. His ships were in a narrow bay of water, somewhat in the same way that the soldiers of Leonidas had been in the narrow valley at Thermopylae. Themistocles, seeing that the Bay of Salamis looked somewhat like the pass at Thermopylae, had an idea. He pretended to be a traitor like the traitor at Thermopylae. He sent word to Xerxes that if one half of the Persian fleet stayed at one end of the strait and the other half closed off the other end of the strait, the Greeks would be penned in between and caught in a trap.

International Visual Aids Center, Belgium

Historical Pictures Service, Chicago

Xerxes thought this was a good idea, so he gave orders to have his ships do as Themistocles had suggested. But Xerxes, smiling on his throne, had the surprise of his life. The result was just the opposite of what he had expected. With the Persian fleet in this narrow strait, the smaller Greek ships could get in between and fight both halves of it separately. The space was so narrow that the big Persian ships couldn't move. They got in the way of each other and rammed and sank their own boats!

And so the Persian fleet was completely beaten. They had lost about two hundred ships. The proud and boastful Xerxes, with most of his army and all that was left of his navy, made a hasty retreat. The Persians once more went back home in disgrace. The amazing, intelligent, and courageous Greeks were again victorious!

One year later—in 479 B.C.—at the town of Plataea, the Greeks conquered what was left of the Persian army—and this was the last time the Persians ever tried to conquer the small land of Greece!

If Themistocles had not built such a strong fleet, what do you think would have become of Athens and Greece?

Although Persian troops did not fight in Greece again, many other battles were fought between the Greeks and Persians. Many Greek cities in other places were attacked by the Persians, and Athens and Sparta helped these cities to defend themselves.

Wars in these times lasted a long time, but this was partly because fighting went on only in good weather. In the winter, even where it didn't snow, armies stopped fighting and waited until spring. If there was no snow, there was rain and mud, and this kind of bad weather made it almost impossible for men to fight.

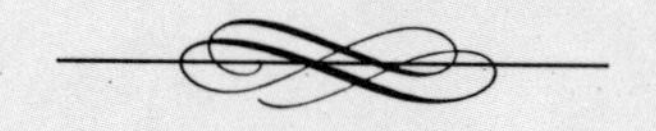

The Golden Age of Pericles

After the wars with Persia, Athens seemed to be cheered up by her victory and began to do wonderful things. The next fifty years—between 480 B.C. and 430 B.C.—were the most wonderful years in the history of Greece. Perhaps they were the most wonderful years in the history of the world. These fifty years are called the Golden Age.

Athens, as you remember, had been burned down by Xerxes. At the time, this seemed like a terrible misfortune. But it wasn't. The people set to work and built a finer and much more beautiful city than the old one had been. The most important person in Athens at this time was a man named Pericles (pair′ih-kleez). He was neither a king nor a ruler, but he was a very wise man and a wonderful speaker. Pericles was such a popular leader that the Athenians always tried to follow his teachings. One of the main things he taught was that every person should work very hard to make the most of himself and his abilities.

Historical Pictures Service, Chicago

Portrait bust of Pericles. Vatican, Rome.

Pericles was like the popular captain of a team who is a fine player himself and can make fine players of all the others on his team. Athens was Pericles' team, and he trained it so well that nearly any member of the team would have been able to fill nearly any position no matter how important it might have been. Some men became great artists, some great writers, and some great philosophers. Philosophers are wise men who know a lot about life because they study it calmly and learn to understand it better than most of us do. They search for knowledge and truth and do their best to pass on to others what they have learned.

Architects built many beautiful buildings in Athens; sculptors made statues of Greek gods and goddesses that were placed on the buildings, in the temples, and in public places throughout the city; and the philosophers taught the people how to think about, discuss, and understand problems, and how to be wise and good.

International Visual Aids Center, Belgium

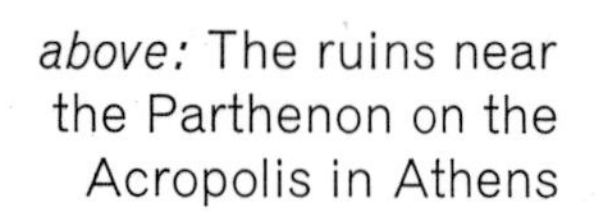

above: The ruins near the Parthenon on the Acropolis in Athens

International Visual Aids Center, Belgium

International Visual Aids Center, Belgium

right, top to bottom:

Stairway of the sacred path that surrounded the Acropolis in Athens

The Erechtheum, Acropolis, Athens

The Odeon Theater, a typical outdoor Greek theater

The Parthenon

The writers of the Golden Age composed such wonderful plays that no playwright since that time has been able to do better! These plays are still performed today—all over the world—and many modern plays are based on the Greek plays. The four greatest Greek playwrights were Aeschylus (es'kih-luss), Sophocles (soff'uh-kleez), Euripides (you-rip'ih-deez), and Aristophanes (air-ih-stoff'ah-neez).

Aeschylus was the first playwright we know of who wrote plays called *tragedies*, which were about problems between men and gods. These plays never had happy endings.

Sophocles is usually called the best writer of Greek tragedies. His plays are perfectly and beautifully written.

In the plays of Euripides the characters seem much more human and true-to-life than the characters in the plays of Aeschylus and Sophocles. Euripides' plays are not quite so serious as the tragedies of the other two playwrights.

Aristophanes wrote funny plays—comedies—about the things that were happening in Athens.

The theaters in Greece were not like most of those we have now. They were always outdoor theaters, usually on the side of a hill, where a "grandstand" could be built facing the stage. There was little or no scenery, and instead of an orchestra of musicians there was a chorus of singers to accompany the actors.

The actors wore false faces—masks—to show what their feelings were. A "comic" mask with a grinning face was worn for a funny, happy, or comic part; a "tragic" mask with a sorrowful face was worn for a sad, unhappy, or tragic role. Perhaps you have seen pictures of these masks, for in some theaters today these same comic and tragic masks are used as decorations.

The city of Athens had been named after the goddess Athena. She was the guardian goddess of Athens, and was supposed to protect the city. The Athenians built a special temple in her honor on the top of the Acropolis (ah-crop'uh-liss), a hill in Athens. They called this temple the Parthenon (par'theh-nahn).

The Parthenon is considered to be the most beautiful building in the world, even though it is now in ruins. In the center of this temple was a huge statue of Athena made of gold and ivory by a sculptor named Phidias (fid'ee-us). We are told that it was the most beautiful statue in the world, just as the Parthenon was the most beautiful building. The statue has disappeared, and no one knows what became of it. One might guess, however, that the gold and ivory tempted thieves, who may have stolen the statue piece by piece.

Phidias made many other statues and friezes for the outside of the Parthenon, but most of these have been carried away and put in museums or have been lost or destroyed.

The statue of Athena and the other sculptures on the Parthenon made Phidias so famous that he was asked to make a statue of Zeus to be placed at Olympia, where the Olympic Games were held. The statue of Zeus was even finer than the one he had made of Athena. It was so splendid that it was called one of the Seven Wonders of the Ancient World.

Democracy was the form of government that developed in Athens during the Golden Age. Democracy means that the people rule. Women, foreigners, and slaves, however, were not allowed to take part in the government affairs of Athens. The government met in the city and the citizens who did have the right to vote and to voice their opinions did so very actively and directly. All males over eighteen could meet in the assembly and vote for or against laws.

In those days there were at times epidemics of a terrible, contagious disease, called the plague (playg). People died by the thousands from the plague, for doctors knew very little about how to cure it. Such a plague came upon Athens during the Peloponnesian War, and many Athenians died. Pericles himself nursed the sick and did all he could for them, but finally he, too, was taken ill with the plague and in 429 B.C. he died. So ended the Golden Age, which has been called the Age of Pericles, in honor of its greatest man.

opposite top: The Palaestra of Olympia, a training school for athletes

---

opposite bottom: The entrance to Olympia

International Visual Aids Center, Belgium

The Peloponnesian War

The Golden Age of Athens, when the city was very powerful, lasted for only fifty years. Why, do you suppose, did it end at all? Was the plague that hit Athens the reason? Or the death of Pericles? These things, of course, weakened Athens, but the main cause of her downfall was a fight.

This time the fight was not between Greece and an outside power, as in the Persian wars. This fight was between two cities in Greece that before this time had been fairly friendly. It was a "family" quarrel between Sparta and Athens.

Even though Athens and Sparta had worked together to free Greece from Persia, they were not united into one power. Quarreling and fighting continued. Finally in 477 B.C. all the Greek cities united. They formed one large unit, and Athens was made the head. This unit was called the Confederacy of Delos, or the Delian League. The Greek city-states were now a strong group that could protect their land from the Persians. Each member sent men, ships, or money to the treasury on the island of Delos.

Because this league had been Athens' idea, and because Athens was in charge of the fleet, the treasury, and everything else that was important, she became the strongest member.

The city-states, however, had not been able to get along before this time, and they didn't change. As soon as the danger of war with other countries was past, some of the city-states wanted to be on their own again. They did not want to be under the rule of Athens and they did not want to send money or men for the league's army.

But Athens did not want the confederacy to break up. So the Athenians used force to keep the league together. Because Athens was so powerful she always won. Or did she? By this time there was no longer a real confederacy. The Greek city-states were no longer joined together freely and willingly. Now the league had become the Athenian

Empire. The city-states were ruled by Athens; and in 454 B.C. the money that had been kept on the island of Delos was moved to Athens. It was no longer used just for the good of the league, but for whatever Athens wanted to use it for. It was just as if Athens were collecting taxes.

The Athenian navy continued to use its ships for overseas trade. As this trade developed, Athens came into competition with two city-states who were allies, or friends—Aegina and Corinth. These two city-states were afraid Athens would take away their trade, so they declared war on Athens. But Athens was so strong that Aegina finally surrendered, and then Athens went after Corinth. At this time, however, Sparta went to the aid of Corinth and the two city-states together had quite a strong army. This was the beginning of the fall of Athens.

Athens fought in Corinth, attacked Sparta and her allies, and even made an attack on Persia! After much fighting, Athens began to lose and in 445 B.C. she made a thirty-year peace treaty with Sparta.

Athens, however, did not keep this peace, but continued fighting and conquering anyone who stood in her way. She attacked colonies of Corinth, and Corinth again asked Sparta to help.

Sparta tried to talk the Athenians into keeping peace, but was unsuccessful. Sparta was in a part of Greece that was called the Peloponnesus. That is why this war between Athens and Sparta was called the Peloponnesian War. It was not only Sparta, but *all* of the Peloponnesus that fought against Athens! This war began in 431 B.C., and lasted twenty-seven years!

At the end of this long and bloody war, both Sparta and Athens were tired and worn out, and the glory of Athens was gone. Both cities tried very hard to get help in their struggles against each other. In 413 B.C. Athens attacked the large and powerful city of Syracuse in Sicily in hopes of winning and using their men to help. Athens not only failed to win, but also lost about 40,000 soldiers and two fleets. Meanwhile Sparta turned to the Greek enemy, Persia, for help. From Persia Sparta received gold, and in return, promised to let Persia conquer Greek cities in Asia Minor.

Athens' strong fleet was finally defeated by the Spartan fleet at Goat's River in 405 B.C. Within a year, in 404 B.C., Athens was starved into surrender. Sparta did not destroy the city, but she did destroy the Athenian Empire. Now Sparta was the leader. All Greece was under her influence. But not for long. The Greek city-states continued to fight against each other, and neither Sparta nor Athens ever amounted to much after this time. Neither city had really won, for the Peloponnesian War had ruined them both, which is what often happens in wars.

All during the Peloponnesian War a man by the name of Socrates (sock′rah-teez) lived in Athens. Many people think he was one of the wisest and best men who ever lived. Socrates was a philosopher and he went about the

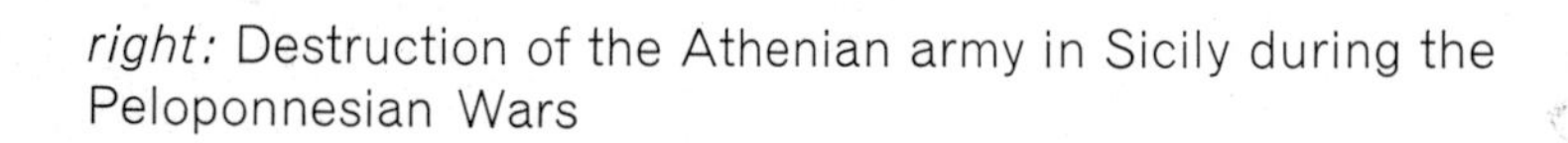

right: Destruction of the Athenian army in Sicily during the Peloponnesian Wars

Historical Pictures Service, Chicago

city teaching the people what he thought was the best way for them to live. But instead of actually telling the people what he thought was right, he asked them questions that made them see for themselves what was right. In this way, mainly by asking questions, he let people find out for themselves what he wanted them to know. This kind of teaching has been called "Socratic" teaching ever since.

Socrates was bald and quite ugly, and yet he was very popular with the Athenians. This may seem strange, for the Athenians loved beautiful faces and beautiful figures and beautiful things, and Socrates was anything but beautiful. It must have been the beauty of Socrates' character that made them forget his ugliness.

International Visual Aids Center, Belgium

above: Portrait bust of Socrates

opposite: Socrates in the streets of Athens

Historical Pictures Service, Chicago

Socrates didn't believe in all the Greek gods, and wanted the Athenians to learn not to believe in them. But he had to be very careful not to actually say he didn't believe in them himself, for the Greeks didn't like anyone to say or do anything against their gods. In fact, a man would have been put to death for teaching young men not to believe in the gods. But Socrates wasn't careful enough to keep his beliefs from becoming well known, and at last he was charged with not believing in the Greek gods and with teaching others not to believe in them. For this he was condemned to death. He was ordered to drink a cup of hemlock, which was a deadly poison. Socrates' pupils, or disciples, as they were then called, tried to have him refuse to drink the cup, but he would not disobey the order. And so, when he was nearly seventy years old, he drank the cup of hemlock and died with all his disciples around him. This was in 399 B.C., four hundred years before Christ was born.

One of the things Socrates believed was that each of us has a conscience that tells us what is right and what is wrong and that we don't have to read from a book or be told by another what is right or what is wrong. Another thing he taught us was that there is a life after death and that when we die our souls live on. No wonder he himself was not afraid to die!

Another man who lived during the Peloponnesian War was the great historian, Thucydides (thoo-sid'ih-deez). He is considered a more accurate historian than Herodotus. Thucydides told about what he saw during the Peloponnesian War. He did not write what other people told him; he wrote what he knew. He is considered the greatest of the ancient historians.

ATHENS

Philip of Macedonia

A man named Philip, who lived north of Greece, had been watching Sparta and Athens fighting in the Peloponnesian War. Philip wanted to get into the game. He was king of a little country called Macedonia (mass-uh-doan'ee-yuh), but he wanted to rule Greece also. It seemed to him that when Sparta and Athens were "down and out" after the Peloponnesian War, the time had come to step in and make himself king of Greece. Philip was a great fighter, but he didn't want to fight Greece unless he had to. He wanted the Greeks to make him king willingly. So he thought up a scheme to bring this about.

Philip knew how the Greeks hated the Persians, whom they had driven out of their country over a hundred years before. Although the Persian Wars had taken place long ago, the Greeks had never forgotten the bravery of their forefathers and the tales of their victories over the Persians. These stories had been told to them over and over by their fathers and grandfathers, and they loved to read and reread them in Herodotus' history.

So Philip said to the Greeks, "Your ancestors drove the Persians out of Greece, to be sure, but the Persians went back to their country, and you didn't go after them and punish them as you should have done. You didn't try to get even with them. Why don't you go over to Persia and conquer it now, and make the Persians pay for what they did to you?" Then he added slyly, "Let me help you. I'll lead you against them."

No one seemed to see through Philip's scheme—no one except one man. This man was an Athenian named Demosthenes (deh-mahs'thuh-neez).

When he was a boy, Demosthenes had decided that he would someday be a great speaker, an orator. But he had picked the one profession which by nature he was worst fitted for. In the first place, he had such a very soft, weak voice that one could hardly hear him. Besides this, he stammered very badly and could not recite even a short poem without hesitating and stumbling so that people laughed at him. It seemed absurd, therefore, that he should try to be a great speaker.

But Demosthenes practiced and practiced by himself. He went down on the seashore and put pebbles in his mouth to make it more difficult to speak clearly. Then he spoke to the roaring waves, making believe that he was addressing an angry crowd who were trying to drown the sound of his voice. He had to speak very loud indeed!

Bob Brunton—Hollis Associates

Alinari-Art Reference Bureau

above left: Demosthenes speaking to the waves

above: Portrait bust of Demosthenes. Galleria Uffizi, Florence.

At last, by constantly practicing, Demosthenes did become the greatest speaker who ever lived. He spoke so wonderfully that he could make his audience laugh or cry whenever he wanted to, and he could persuade people to do almost anything he wished.

Demosthenes was the man who saw through Philip's scheme for conquering Persia. He knew that Philip's real aim was to become king of Greece. So he made twelve speeches against Philip. So famous were they that even today we call a speech that bitterly attacks anyone a "Philippic."

The Greeks who heard the speeches were very much against Philip while they were listening to Demosthenes. But as soon as they got away from the sound of Demosthenes' words, these same Greeks forgot them and did nothing to stop Philip until it was too late. In the battle of Chaeronea (care-uh-nee′uh) in 338 B.C., Philip defeated the Athenians. He became the master of all Greece, just as Demosthenes had warned he would.

But in 336 B.C., before he could conquer Persia, King Philip was killed by one of his own men. Philip had a son named Alexander, however, and although Alexander was only twenty years old when his father died, he became king of both Macedonia and Greece.

Alexander the Great

When Alexander was a child, he saw some men trying without success to tame a young and very wild horse that shied and reared in the air so that no one was able to ride him. Alexander asked to be allowed to try to ride the animal. His father made fun of Alexander for wanting to attempt what those older than he had been unable to do, but at last gave his consent.

Alexander had noticed something the others had not noticed. The horse seemed to be afraid of his own shadow. Young colts are often frightened by anything black and moving, just as some children are afraid of the dark.

Alexander knew this and turned the horse around so he faced the sun. This way the shadow was out of the horse's sight. Alexander then mounted the animal, and to the amazement of all, rode off without any further trouble!

His father was delighted at Alexander's cleverness and gave him the horse, as a reward. Alexander named the horse Bucephalus (bew-sef′a-lus) and became so fond of him that when the horse died, Alexander built a monument to him.

Alexander was indeed a clever boy. And he had a wonderful teacher named Aristotle (air′iss-taht-el). Aristotle's teacher had been named Plato. Plato's teacher had been Socrates. Many people think that at least part of Alexander's greatness was due to Aristotle.

Aristotle wrote many books about many different things, including stars, animals, politics, and plays.

For thousands of years these books that Aristotle wrote were the school books that boys and girls studied, and for a thousand years they were the *only* school books. These days, a school book is usually out-of-date a very short time after it is written, and is then no longer used. So you can see how remarkable it was that Aristotle's school books should have been used for so long a time.

Even though Alexander was king of both Macedonia and Greece, his kingdom was too small for him. He wanted to carry out his father's plans. But he wanted to do even more. He wanted to bring all people together into a world civilization. You see, Aristotle had taught him to understand that all people, with their different religions and art and learning, were important and their knowledge should be shared.

So Alexander went ahead with the plan to conquer Persia. The time had come to pay Persia back for that last invasion, which had happened one hundred and fifty years before.

Alexander got together his army and in 334 B.C. crossed the Hellespont into Asia Minor. Here he won battle after battle against the first Persian armies sent out to stop him. Although Alexander's army was small, his soldiers had had excellent training from Philip, and Alexander was a great general. He was daring and brave. Some of his battle plans were so well planned and organized that they are studied even today by military men as models to follow and learn from.

Alinari-Art Reference Bureau

opposite: Alexander the Great on his horse, Bucephalus

above: Statue of Alexander's teacher, Aristotle. Spada Gallery, Rome.

Alexander kept moving on, for Persia was a vast empire. A temple in one town he came to contained a rope tied into a very famous and puzzling knot. It was called the Gordian Knot, and it was famous because an oracle had said that whoever should undo this knot would conquer Persia. But no one had ever been able to untie it.

When Alexander heard the story, he went to the temple and looked at the knot. He saw at once that it would be impossible to untie it, so instead of even trying as others had done, he drew his sword and with one stroke cut the knot in two.

From that time on, Alexander conquered one city after another and never lost a battle. At the battle of Arbela in 331 B.C., Alexander defeated the army of Darius III and conquered Persia.

In 330 B.C. Alexander went into Egypt, which also belonged to Persia, and conquered that country, too. To celebrate this victory, Alexander founded a town near the mouth of the Nile River and named it Alexandria, after himself. There he started a great library in which there were later said to be five hundred thousand books. That is half a million books! It was the largest library of ancient times. The books were not like the kind we have now, of course, for printing had not been invented. Every one of these ancient books was written *by hand* on long sheets of papyrus that were rolled up on sticks to form a scroll.

In the harbor of this town of Alexandria was a little island called Pharos. On this island some years later a remarkable lighthouse was built. The lighthouse of Pharos

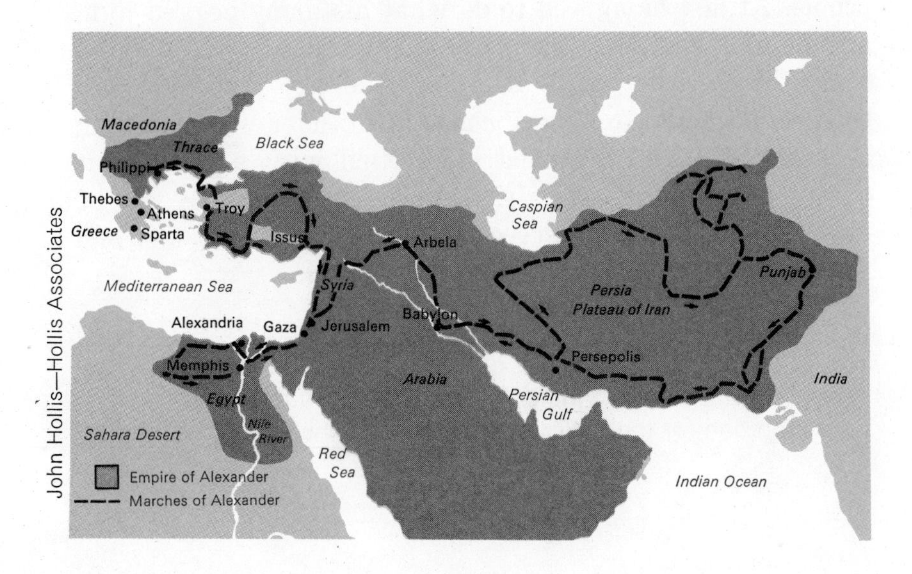

John Hollis—Hollis Associates

opposite: Portrait bust of Alexander the Great

left: The Empire of Alexander the Great

looked like a modern skyscraper with a tower. It was over thirty stories high—which was most remarkable because at that time most buildings were only one or two stories high. The Pharos could be seen for miles because it was so high. The lighthouse was named the Pharos of Alexandria and was called one of the Seven Wonders of the Ancient World.

Alexandria grew to be the largest and most important seaport and place of learning in the ancient world. Now, however, the Pharos and the library and all the old buildings have disappeared, but the city is still important.

Alexander did not stay in one place for very long. He was restless and wanted to continue with his plan for conquering and uniting the peoples of the world. Alexander kept on conquering until he had reached far-off India.

In India the men in Alexander's army, which had stayed with him all the way, became homesick. They had been away from home for more than ten years and were so far away that they were afraid they would never get back.

Alexander was now only thirty years old, but he was called Alexander the Great, for he was ruler of most of the world that was then known to be inhabited by civilized people. At last he agreed to do what his army begged him, and he started slowly back toward Greece.

By the time he got to Babylon—the city that had once been so large and so magnificent—Alexander was sick with a fever. Still he celebrated his return with a feast; but during his feasting and drinking he died suddenly. So he never did get back to Greece. This was in 323 B.C., when Alexander was only thirty-three years old.

---

opposite: King Porus of India inspects his elephant corps in preparation for the invasion of Alexander the Great

Alexander the Great had conquered the Persian Empire. He had governed the largest territory under the rule of one man, and had held on to his hope of uniting the world—a hope that most of the people in the world today still hold.

Alexander was not only a great ruler and a great general, but also a great teacher. Alexander taught the Greek language to the people he conquered so that they could read Greek books. He taught them the wise sayings of the Greek philosophers—Socrates, Plato, and Aristotle. He taught them about Greek sculpture and painting. He trained the people in athletics, just the way the Greeks trained for their Olympic Games. And so we can say that in a way he taught far more people than any other teacher who has ever lived.

He helped unite these peoples by encouraging marriages between members of different groups and respect for different ways of living and different religions.

Alexander had married a beautiful Persian princess named Roxana, but their son was not born until after Alexander's death. When Alexander died there was no one in his family who could rule. At one time, he had told his generals that after his death the strongest one of them should be the next ruler. To determine the strongest, he said, they should fight it out among themselves.

His generals did fight to see who should win, and finally the three who were the strongest decided to divide the empire among themselves.

One of the winners was named Ptolemy I (tahl'eh-mee). He took Egypt as his share and ruled well. But the other two did not amount to much, and soon their shares became unimportant and went to pieces. Like a balloon that stretches and stretches as you blow it up, Alexander's empire grew bigger and bigger until—all of a sudden—"pop." Nothing was left but the pieces.

But don't you wonder what it would have been like if Alexander had ruled for longer than only thirteen years?

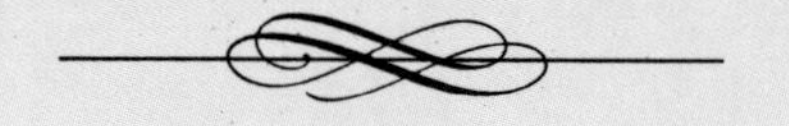

The First Punic War: Rome Begins to Expand

In many ways the same thing happens with countries that happens with people. One country wins the championship from another, holds it for a few years, and then loses it to a newcomer.

We have seen that Ninevah was champion for awhile; then Babylon had her turn; then Persia had her turn; then Greece; and lastly Macedonia.

You may wonder who was to be the next champion after Alexander's empire went to pieces—who was to have the next turn.

When Alexander was conquering the world he went east, toward the rising sun, and south. He paid little attention to Rome—to the west of Macedonia, toward the setting sun.

Rome, after forming a government that included the plebeians, fought many wars. Up until the time Philip of Macedonia conquered Greece, Rome spent most of her time defending herself from her enemies; that is, from 450 B.C. to about 338 B.C.

But about the time of Alexander's death, Rome began to expand and conquer other towns in Italy. Between 325 and 290 B.C. Rome conquered the south-central part of Italy. In the southern part of Italy were Greek city-states whose people happened to be quarreling among themselves. In 281 B.C., Rome attempted to invade Tarentum, the biggest Greek city in Italy. But the people of Tarentum called for help from Pyrrhus (peer′ us)—a relative of Alexander the Great—and he came to their aid.

Pyrrhus used a type of warfare the Romans had never seen. He had elephants in his army that broke lines and scattered soldiers. Although Rome was being beaten in battle, Pyrrus knew that in time Rome would win. He sent a great speaker to a meeting of the Roman senate to persuade the Romans to sign a peace treaty. The Romans said no! As long as there were Greek soldiers on Roman soil, they would keep on fighting. Finally Rome captured Tarentum and forced the other Greek city-states to come under Roman rule. By 270 B.C. Rome ruled the lands from the Po Valley in the north all the way to the tip of the boot in the south.

During these long years of fighting, Rome at first just defended herself against her enemies, but later used her power to conquer other lands and people. Rome built up a citizen-army. The soldiers who fought for Rome were well trained and well organized. An average legion had 5,000 soldiers who could fight as one big group or in smaller units. The officers and commanders of the army were men who had had experience, and they knew how to train and lead men.

The Roman soldiers wore helmets and armor and carried shields. They used spears seven feet long, swords, and broad swords. Cavalry—soldiers on horseback—helped the foot soldiers.

Just as a disobedient or cowardly soldier was punished, sometimes by death, a brave and loyal soldier was rewarded. If a man saved the life of a fellow soldier in battle he was given a crown of oak leaves, which was considered the highest honor.

After a successful campaign, the soldiers would march gloriously through Rome up to the Temple of Jupiter, which was on a hill. The commander, dressed in purple robes, rode in a grand chariot in front of long lines of captured soldiers. The citizens of Rome then cheered and applauded their brave and victorious army.

By 270 B.C. all the towns and states in Italy were ruled by Rome. Once Rome had gained control of an area she was very just. She allowed the people to keep their own government, religion, and law as long as they cooperated with her. They had to follow where Rome led in battle and had to send troops or money to help fight Rome's enemies.

In Alexander's time, Rome had been only a small town with narrow streets and frame houses—not nearly important enough for Alexander to think much about. But now Rome set to work and built roads. These roads were like paved streets. Large rocks were placed at the bottom for a foundation, smaller stones placed on top, and large, flat paving stones were laid over this base. Thousands of miles of such roads were built to all parts of Italy. Later they were built to all parts of the empire. One could go from

Historical Pictures Service, Chicago

above: A Roman soldier

opposite: Roman soldiers

almost anywhere all the way to Rome on paved roads. We still use the expression, "All roads lead to Rome." So well were these roads made that many of them exist today, two thousand years after they were built!

These roads were built for military and economic reasons. Troops and supplies could move much faster along these roads, messages could be sent much faster, and merchants could carry their wares from town to town.

In spite of the expression about all roads leading *into* Rome, the roads were originally intended to lead *out of* Rome—carrying troops. The first road built was called *Via Appia*, which is Latin for Appian Way. It goes south from Rome and still exists today, though it is not called just *Via Appia*, but *Via Appia Antica*. "Antica" means "very old." Other roads lead out in other directions from Rome.

Perhaps you have noticed on the map that Italy looks like a "boot" that is about to kick a little island. This island is Sicily. Just opposite Sicily, across the Mediterranean Sea in Africa, was a city called Carthage.

Historical Pictures Service, Chicago

Carthage was a city-state located on the best harbor of the southern shore of the Mediterranean Sea—on the coast of Africa. Trade was the most important occupation. Carthage traded with Egyptians and Phoenicians and became very wealthy. Because the land was so fertile, it produced all the food necessary for the existence of the people, plus extra grain, figs, wine, and olive oil. The extra grain, figs, and wine were the things the Carthaginians used in trade. The Carthaginians didn't have many colonies, but they had many trading posts.

Carthage ruled part of Sicily at this time, and when a local war started there in 264 B.C. Rome decided to fight Carthage for control of the island. This would be the first time that Roman soldiers had fought outside their own land. But this was to be just the beginning—Roman troops were to fight with Carthage in many other lands, including Spain and Africa.

The conflict between the two powers for land and power was to continue—off and on—for the unbelievable period of 119 years!

The first war between Carthage and Rome lasted from 264 B.C. to 241 B.C. It was called the *First Punic War*. The word "punic" (pyou′ nick), comes from a Latin word meaning "Carthaginian" or "Phoenician."

Bob Brunton—Hollis Associates

Though Rome had an excellent citizen-army with good, disciplined troops, she realized very early in the war that without ships she could never hope to win. Rome would have to fight the Carthaginians on the sea, for Carthage had such a strong navy that she ruled the Mediterranean. But the Romans had no boats. Their city was not on the seashore, and they knew nothing about making boats, nor about sailing them, even if they had had them. The Carthaginians, on the other hand, had many boats, and like the Phoenicians, were experienced sailors.

Rome happened to find the wreck of a Carthaginian ship that had been cast ashore, and the people at once set to work to make a copy of it. In a very short time—some records say sixty days—she had built one ship, then another and another, until she had a great many ships. While the ships were being built, men were trained to row them. Then, though she was new at the game, Rome attacked the Carthaginian fleet.

The kind of boats used at this time were called *quinqueremes*. Instead of having three rows of oars on each side as the triremes had had, the quinqueremes had four or five banks of oars. These ships were made for ramming other ships.

It would seem that the Carthaginians could have won easily, since the Romans knew so little about boats. The Roman ships were made for ramming, smashing, and sinking the enemy ships, and much skill was needed in handling them.

The Romans knew they were no match for the Carthaginians in this sort of fighting. So they thought of a way in which they could fight the way they might fight on land.

International Visual Aids Center, Belgium

opposite top: Victorious Roman soldiers marching through a triumphal arch toward the Temple of Jupiter

opposite bottom: An early Roman road. All that remains is the base layer of rocks.

They invented a big hook that they placed at the prow—the front—of the ship. This hook was called a *crow*. A Roman ship was supposed to run alongside a Carthaginian ship, and throw out this crow. The hook would crash into the deck and pull the other ship right up close to the Roman ship and hold the two together. The Roman soldiers would then scramble over the sides into the enemy's boat and fight them the same way they would fight on land.

The scheme worked. This great sea fight took place in about 260 B.C. at Mylae (my′ lee), and it was a very important battle because only by sea power would Rome be able to rule the Mediterranean.

This new kind of fighting took the Carthaginians by surprise, and at first they were no match for the Romans. Rome was victorious in the battle itself, but the Romans were such poor sailors that many ships were lost and much money was spent building new ones. In one storm alone, Rome lost 117 ships and 20,000 men!

The Roman army invaded and attacked the city of Carthage, but were at first defeated by Carthaginian armies using foot soldiers and charging elephants. But Rome was determined that she would not give up. About 15,000 Roman soldiers were killed, and Regulus, a Roman consul, was captured. The Carthaginians sent Regulus back to Rome, because he promised to persuade the Romans to make peace. When Regulus came to Rome, however, he told the people to keep on attacking, because Carthage was becoming very weak. Regulus had been defeated in Carthage because he had made mistakes, but even so he became a hero. He had told the Carthaginians that if Rome was not going to stop the war he would return as their prisoner. Regulus kept his word. He did return and was killed by the Carthaginians.

Shortly after that, in 241 B.C., Rome was victorious and demanded very hard peace terms. After suffering through twenty-four years of war she did not want Carthage to become strong enough to begin another war. Rome made the people of Carthage promise to pay her four million dollars during the next twenty years. Rome also took the island of Sicily for her own. Thus ended the First Punic War.

right: The Romans and the Carthaginians at Mylae during the First Punic War.

Historical Pictures Service, Chicago

Alinari-Art Reference Bureau

Portrait bust of Hannibal. Museo Nazionale, Naples.

Hannibal and the Second Punic War

After her defeat by Rome, Carthage was faced with the problem of finding the money Rome demanded she pay. By the time the war had ended, Carthage didn't have even enough money to pay her troops. So she decided to mine gold and silver in Spain to raise money. A general named Hamilcar Barca was sent to run the mines. Not only did Hamilcar develop mining for Carthage, but also—with the help of his son, Hannibal, and his son-in-law, Hasdrubal—he started training a new army made up of Spanish tribesmen.

The Romans learned what was happening and knew that Carthage was recovering from the war and again had become wealthy and powerful.

Hannibal, the son of Hamilcar, became a fine soldier and was determined to defeat Rome in battle. He attacked and captured a city in Spain that he knew was friendly with Rome, for he was sure that Rome would fight a war to free the city. When Rome learned that Hannibal had captured one of her allies in Spain, she was afraid that he might go on to conquer more of the country. Rome immediately sent a fleet to Spain to free the captured city and to try to stop Hannibal from gaining any more territory.

At about the same time the Roman fleet set out for Spain, Hannibal and his army began an overland march to Rome. The lands of Spain, Gaul (now called France), and Italy curve around the Mediterranean Sea in the shape of a half-moon, or semicircle. Italy forms the eastern shore of the Mediterranean, and Spain forms the western shore. The land with the northern coastline of the Mediterranean was Gaul. Across the top of Italy's "boot" are the mighty mountains called the Alps. They are miles high and even in summer are covered with ice and snow. There are steep cliffs with narrow ledges on which a man walking must be very, very careful, for if he made a single misstep, he would be dashed to death thousands of feet below.

Nevertheless, Hannibal set out with his men, elephants, and all his supplies on the semicircular route that would lead through Spain and Gaul and over the high and dangerous Alps into Italy. Rome believed that the Alps formed a natural "wall" that was rugged enough to keep anyone out of their country—a much better wall than any city could possibly build! The Romans were sure that it would be impossible for an army to climb over such a very high and dangerous mountain range.

Historical Pictures Service, Chicago

Hannibal landing in Spain

When the Roman fleet arrived at a seaport in Gaul on their way to Spain, they heard that Hannibal's army was just a little north of them and was traveling by land. The Romans tried to overtake Hannibal, but he took his army farther north, and they missed him. So the Romans sent part of the fleet on to Spain and the rest went back to Genoa, a northern Italian town on the seacoast, to wait for Hannibal.

Hannibal managed the amazing feat of leading his army across the Alps, but he lost many of his men during the difficult crossing. By the time he entered the Po Valley, on the other side of the Alps, he had lost half his men. To make up for the loss, he hired Gauls as soldiers, and more troops from Spain. Hannibal was a great general, and had no trouble at all handling a mixed army made up of Carthaginians, Spaniards, and Gauls.

Hannibal crossing the Alps

Bob Brunton—Hollis Associates

Rome, on the other hand, had no good generals, and although the Roman soldiers were good fighters, they hadn't fought for a long time and were not in very good condition. The Romans were unable to keep Hannibal from marching on toward their city, winning battle after battle as he came along. Hannibal marched up and down Italy, conquering other towns in the land and doing pretty much as he pleased.

In one clever maneuver, at the battle of Lake Trasimeno (traz-ih-men'oh), Hannibal succeeded in moving his army between two Roman armies who were after him. He destroyed an army of about forty thousand men. This was one of the greatest ambushes in all history.

It seemed that the only safe place for Romans was Rome. The Romans tried electing a dictator. But Fabius (fay'bee-us), the man they elected, did nothing as Hannibal continued to destroy all the land that Rome controlled. Soon the Romans could no longer stand by and watch their land being taken from them, so they removed Fabius from his office and returned their consuls to power. Now they were going to fight.

The two armies met at the town of Cannae (can'ee) in 216 B.C. When the Romans attacked the Carthaginian line, Hannibal had the middle of his line fall back. The Romans thought they were winning and pushed forward. But Hannibal was smart. Soon the Romans had pushed the middle of Hannibal's line so far back that the two sides of that army could close in. The Roman army was in the middle and Hannibal could attack from both sides. Then the cavalry charged from the rear. There had been eighty-five thousand soldiers in the Roman army, and only about fifteen thousand survived this battle. So many leaders were killed that Rome had to elect 173 new senators!

Hannibal tried to persuade the people of Italy to join his army and fight against Rome. Some people of the southern cities did just that, but most of the people remained loyal to Rome.

Syracuse, in Sicily, went against Rome, and Rome sent a fleet to try to regain control of the town. A famous Greek scientist named Archimedes (ark-ih-meed'eez), lived in Syracuse at the time. He is famous for finding what we call *pi* a number that is used to find the circumference of a circle—that is, the distance around a circle. This man had wonderful ideas to help keep Rome away from Syracuse. Syracuse was a city on the seacoast with high walls around it. Archimedes had the people build on the walls huge cranes that would swing out and drop gigantic stones on the ships. Hooks and pulleys lifted the ships from the water and then dropped them again so they sank. Still the Romans kept fighting, hoping to reconquer Sicily. But Rome really wanted more than Sicily. She wanted to defeat Hannibal's Carthaginian army once and for all.

Now, in some games, if you can't defend your own goal, it may be a good plan to try attacking your opponent's goal. Sometimes the best defense is a good offense.

Rome thought she would try this plan, and decided to attack Carthage, while Hannibal was attacking her. Rome sent a young man named Scipio (sip′ee-oh) to lead the attack.

First, however, Scipio went to Spain to cut off Hannibal from the way he had come and from the first supply of soldiers. For although Hannibal had not lost a battle he had lost men. Then Scipio went over the sea to Africa to attack Carthage itself. The Carthaginians, frightened at being attacked while their general and his army were far off in Italy, sent for Hannibal to come home as fast as he could. But when at last he arrived, it was too late. Scipio defeated Hannibal's army at the town of Zama, near Carthage. That battle, in 201 B.C., ended the Second Punic War. This war had lasted sixteen years.

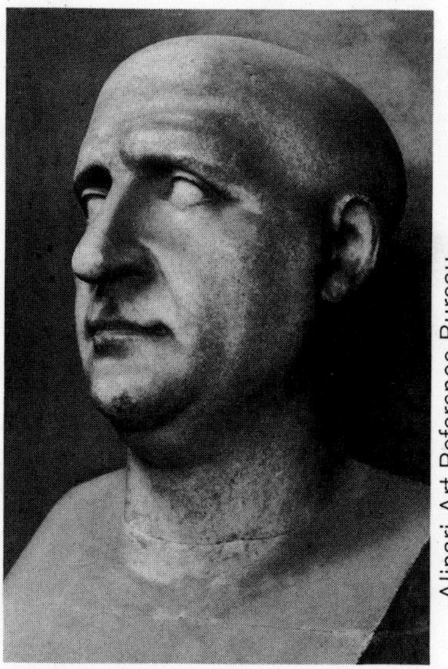
Alinari-Art Reference Bureau

Portrait bust of Scipio. Villa Albani, Rome.

The Romans had won two wars against Carthage, but still they weren't satisfied. The Romans thought they had not beaten Carthage badly enough. They were afraid she was not quite dead or that she might come to life and start fighting again.

Peace with Carthage lasted until 149 B.C., when Rome started the Third Punic War by attacking Carthage. This war lasted until 146 B.C. when the Romans defeated Carthage completely.

The Romans burned the city to the ground and sold the Carthaginians who survived into slavery. It is said the Romans even plowed over the land so that no trace of the city should remain, and that they sowed it with salt so that nothing more would grow there. After that, Carthage was never rebuilt, and now it is hard to tell where the old city once was. Africa became a province ruled by Rome.

Courtesy of the Smithsonian Institution, Freer Gallery of Art, Washington, D.C.

above: A page from a 4th-5th century Greek manuscript of *The Four Gospels.* The manuscript was written on parchment and bound in painted board covers.

---

opposite: A portrait bust of Aristotle, the Greek philosopher who was the teacher of Alexander the Great.

International Visual Aids Center, Belgium

International Visual Aids Center, Belgium

Bob Brunton—Hollis Associates

above: A Greek terracotta vase

---

right: Artisans in ancient Greece at work making pottery

Ruins of the Temple at Delphi where the Delphic Oracle made her prophesies

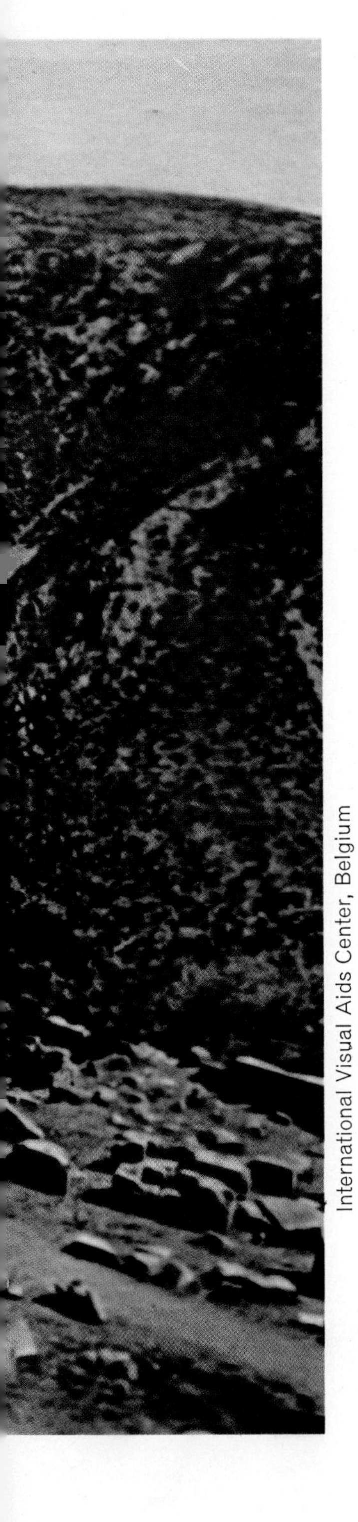

International Visual Aids Center, Belgium

Bob Brunton—Hollis Associates

The Delphic Oracle

International Visual Aids Center, Belgium

International Visual Aids Center, Belgium

above: A view of the country at Marathon where the Greeks defeated the huge Persian army

---

opposite: A Greek terracotta head

Bob Brunton—Hollis Associates

A trireme, the ship with three rows of oars like the ones King Darius of Persia used to carry his army over the sea to Greece.

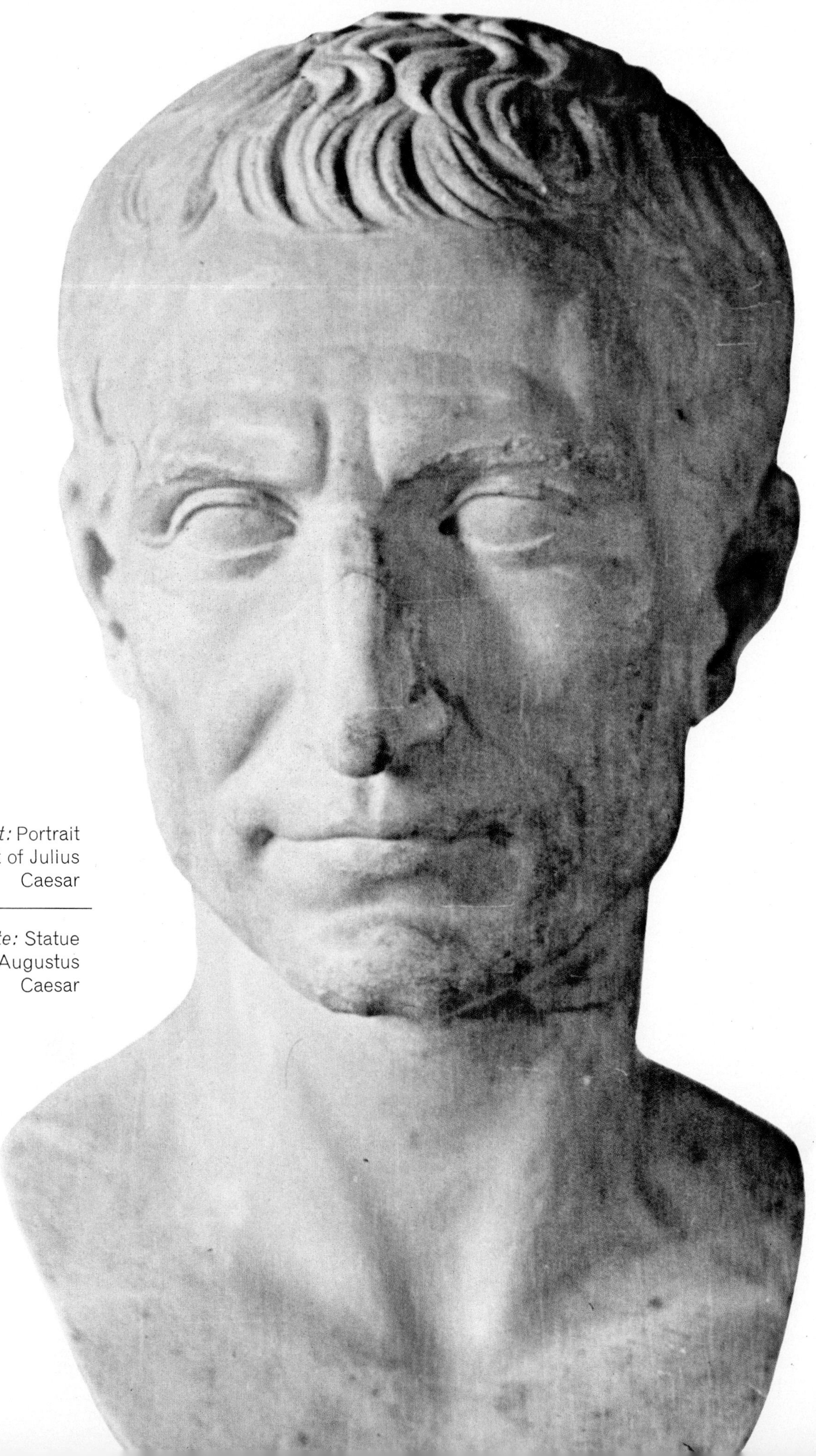

right: Portrait bust of Julius Caesar

opposite: Statue of Augustus Caesar

International Visual Aids Center, Belgium

International Visual Aids Center, Belgium

The Metropolitan Museum of Art, Samuel D. Lee Fund, 1940

International Visual Aids Center, Belgium

opposite: Portrait head of the Emperor Caracalla, who ruled Rome in the 3rd century A.D.

above: Relief of two Roman chariot horses. The artist may have put wings on the horses to show the speed with which they could run.

International Visual Aids Center, Belgium

International Visual Aids Center, Belgium

International Visual Aids Center, Belgium

opposite top: Roman colored glass vases

opposite bottom: Roman gold jewelry

left: Portrait bust of the Emperor Nero

International Visual Aids Center, Belgium

Early Roman gold coins

Field Museum of Natural History, Chicago

A painting on wood of a woman mummy. The portrait, found in Egypt, was made during the Roman period in the 2nd century A.D.

Rome Rules the Mediterranean

You can imagine how proud all the Romans now were, for Rome was ruler not only of Italy, but of Spain and Africa too. Like other nations before her, once she had started conquering, Rome kept on conquering. By 100 B.C. she, in her turn, was ruler of nearly all the countries bordering the Mediterranean Sea—all except Egypt.

The new champion of the world was to be champion for a great many years because she was very businesslike and practical.

The Greeks loved beautiful things—beautiful buildings, beautiful sculpture, and beautiful poems. The Romans copied the Greeks who lived in southern Italy and Sicily and learned from them how to make many beautiful things. The Romans, however, were most interested in useful things.

The Romans showed their practical minds by making two very important city improvements. Nowadays, if you live in a city, you turn on a faucet and get plenty of pure water whenever you want it. The people in cities at that time, however, usually had to get their water both for drinking and for washing from wells or springs nearby. These springs and wells often became dirty and made the people very sick. And so every so often because of such dirty water, there were terrible plagues. You remember the one in Athens, when people died faster than they could be buried.

The Romans wanted fresh water, so they set to work to find lakes from which they could get it. The lakes were often many miles away from the city, so the Romans then built big pipes to carry the water to the city. This pipe was not made of iron or clay as it usually is today, but of stone and concrete; it was called an *aqueduct*, which in Latin means "water carrier." If an aqueduct had to cross a river or a valley, the Romans built a bridge to hold it up. Many of the Roman aqueducts are still standing, and some are in use even now.

International Visual Aids Center, Belgium

A Roman aqueduct

Until this time, waste water and every other kind of dirt and refuse were simply dumped into the street. This naturally made the Roman cities and towns filthy and very unhealthy and was another cause of plagues. But now the Romans built great underground sewers to carry off this dirt and waste water and empty it someplace where it would do no harm and cause no sickness. Nowadays, every large city has aqueducts and sewers, and we take them for granted, but the Romans were the first to build them on a large scale.

One of the most important things that Rome did was to make rules that everyone had to obey. We call these rules laws. Many of these rules were so fair and just that some modern laws are taken from them.

All the cities and towns of the Roman Empire had to pay taxes to Rome. So Rome became the richest city in the world. She spent millions putting up beautiful buildings and monuments in the city—temples to gods, public buildings called basilicas, public baths, and huge open-air places called circuses and amphitheaters.

Chariot races were held in the Circus Maximus, which was a huge racecourse, and thousands of Romans enjoyed watching these races often.

The amphitheaters were something like athletic fields or stadiums. In them were held deadly fights between men, or between men and animals. But the sport that the Romans enjoyed most of all was a fight of gladiators (glad'ee-ay-torz). The word "gladiator" is the Latin word for "sword." Gladiators were very strong and powerful men who had been captured in battle by the Romans and were truly fighters or "swords." They were made to fight with one another or with wild animals for the amusement of the crowd. These gladiatorial fights were very cruel, but the Romans enjoyed seeing bloodshed. It amused them to see one man kill another man or a wild animal. Usually the gladiators fought until one or the other was killed, for the people usually were not satisfied until this happened.

Sometimes, however, if a gladiator who had been knocked out had shown himself to be particularly brave, a good fighter, or a good sport, the people seated all around the amphitheater would turn their thumbs up as a sign that his life was to be spared by the other gladiator. So the winning gladiator, before killing his opponent, would wait to see what the people wished. If they turned their thumbs down, it meant he was to finish the fight by killing the man.

Rome had become a fine, beautiful, and healthy city in which to live, but not for everyone. The rich people were getting richer from the money that came from all over the empire, while the poor people—who got nothing—were getting poorer and poorer all the time. The people conquered by the Romans in battle were brought to Rome. The Romans made slaves of them and sold them to the rich who worked them without pay. It is said that at least half of all the people in Rome were slaves.

opposite top: A fight to the death between two gladiators

opposite bottom: A Roman chariot race

Bob Brunton—Hollis Associates

Statue of a Roman pugilist, or fighter. Museo Nazionale delle Terme, Rome.

At this time in Rome lived the great General Scipio, who had conquered Hannibal in the Second Punic War. Scipio had a daughter named Cornelia Gracchus (grak′us), who had two sons called Tiberius and Gaius. They were very fine boys, and Cornelia was very proud of them.

When they grew up, Cornelia's sons—the Gracchi (grak′eye) as they were called—saw such great extravagance among the rich and such great misery among the poor in Rome that they wanted to do something about it. They became tribunes to represent the people. They saw that the poor had hardly anything to eat and no place to live because the rich kept buying up all the farmland. This did not seem fair, and the Gracchi tried to lower the price of food so that the poor might be able to buy enough to eat. Then they tried to find some way for these people to have at least a small piece of land where they might raise a few vegetables. They were partly successful in bringing this about. But the people who had great wealth—most of them were senators—didn't like giving up anything to the poor. And so these wealthy Romans killed one of the Gracchi brothers, and later killed the other one. These murders of Cornelia's sons began a hundred years of revolution and civil war that in 30 B.C. finally ended the Roman republic.

The trouble between the wealthy and the poor continued. The plebeians were unhappy with their government, for they felt it did not do enough for them. The aristocrats were running the government. These men, many of whom were members of the senate, thought only of protecting their wealth, keeping the plebeians in their places, and gaining more and more power. So the plebeians and the aristocrats were always working and fighting against each other to get their own way.

Scandals broke out in Rome when it was learned that wealthy government officials were filling their own pockets with the taxes collected in provinces rather than sending the money to Rome. This made the plebeians very angry. But they became even angrier when they found out that officials were able to do this because they had bribed some of the senators.

Now just about this time, the people had a chance to make the senate listen to them. On the northern frontier of Italy a barbarian tribe had been plundering and killing. The senate had sent armies to defeat these barbarians, but each time the armies had been beaten. The situation was

very bad. The victorious barbarians were moving farther down the peninsula, and something had to be done. The plebeians acted. They elected a consul to lead their army. This man was not an aristocrat like the others had been, but a professional soldier. His name was Marius.

Marius succeeded in conquering the barbarian tribes. In doing so he became a popular hero. The people of Rome elected him consul again and again, in spite of the fact that the laws of the republic said that a man could be consul for only one year.

Marius, like the Gracci brothers before him, gained control of the government because he had the support of the plebeians. He was able to keep the consulship for a long time because he had one other thing. He was the general of an army that supported him.

Before the rule of Marius, the Roman army had been made up largely of the small landowners who had to leave their farms to fight. But as the years passed, there were fewer and fewer farmers. The farmlands were taken over by the wealthy who did not want to leave their land to fight in long wars. But Marius changed all this. He opened army service to any volunteers who wanted to join. It didn't matter whether they owned land or not. This gave the poor landless people a good chance. They entered the army for pay and for the land that the general, Marius, promised to give them if they were victorious.

This was an important change in Roman history. Now the soldiers in the Roman army were loyal not to the state, which was run largely by the senate, but to their own general. If *he* were successful *they* would be successful. If their general should fail, the soldiers would not receive what he had promised them. Remember that these men were professional soldiers and had no farms to return to.

From this time on we will see how the army began to play a more active role in the affairs of government. Within a few years Rome was to be taken over forcibly by an army.

This is how it happened. Rome held land in Africa, Asia Minor, and Greece. To keep this land she had to protect it constantly from revolts and outside enemies. In the East

left: Relief showing the Romans fighting the barbarians

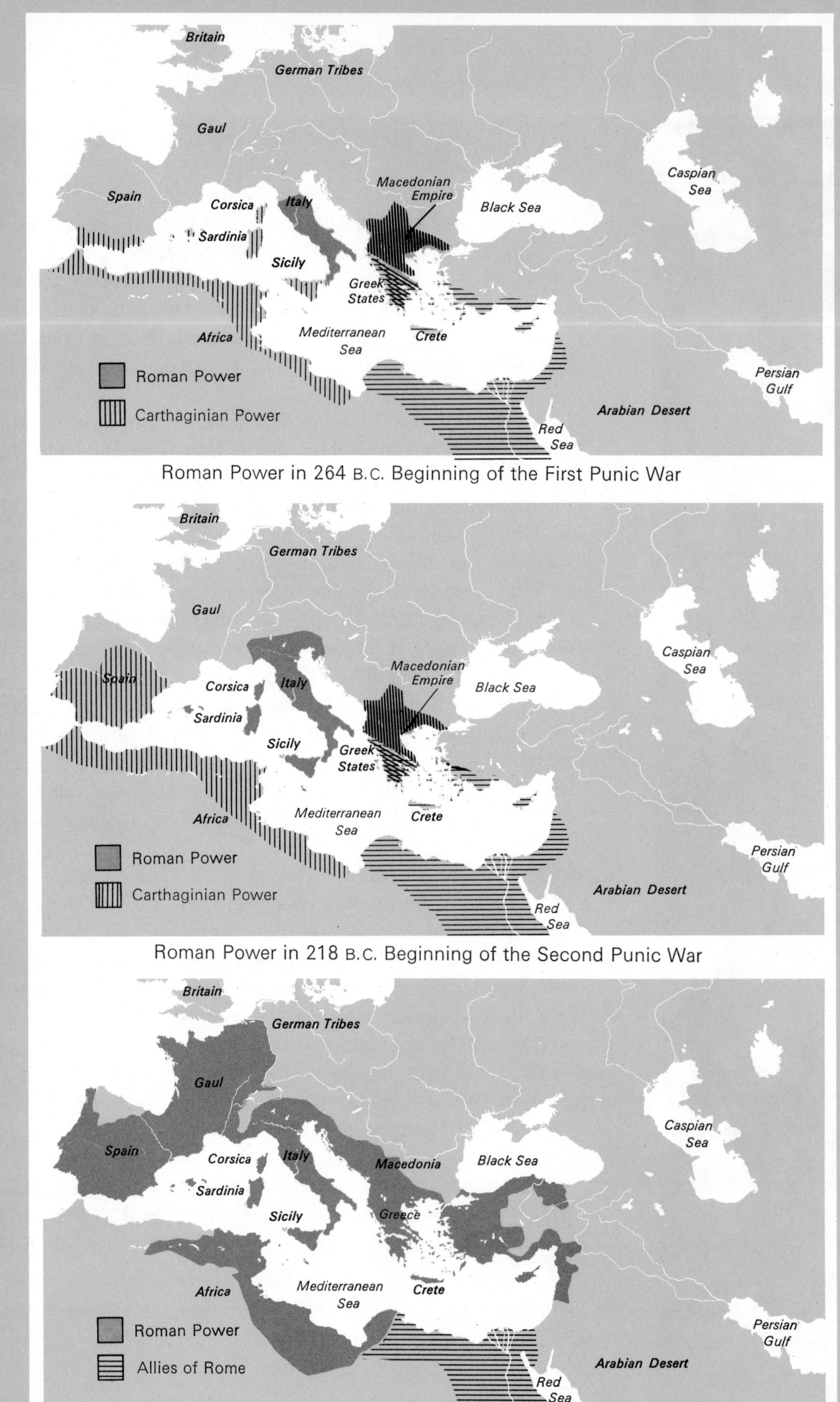

Expansion of the Roman Empire from 264 B.C. to the death of Caesar.

there was a king who invaded and took over some Roman cities in Greece and Asia Minor. To meet this threat, the Roman senate elected an aristocratic consul named Sulla to lead the army. This was the legal way to select a general, but the leaders of the plebeians did not like Sulla and they did not want him to lead their army. So the assembly of the people picked Marius instead.

Sulla was very angry. He decided to force the people to accept him as their leader. He brought his loyal troops to Rome and won the brief fight that took place.

Sulla, backed by his soldiers, took over the city. He drove Marius into exile and made the senate agree to obey his command. Then he went to the East to fight the enemy king.

While Sulla was gone from Rome, Marius gathered his own loyal soldiers and marched on the city. He took Rome and punished his enemies by putting them to death. For the second time Rome had been captured by soldiers who used force to dictate who should be consul.

Soon after Marius had been made consul, however, he died. The government was back in the hands of the senate—but not for long. During this brief period of Marius' last rule, Sulla was leading a victorious army in the East. But in 82 B.C. he returned to Rome leading his well-trained, well-armed, experienced soldiers. He marched on Rome, captured the city, and became a military dictator. This meant that he was the leader of the army and had unlimited power to make laws and punish his enemies.

Then Sulla began to change Roman law. He had ignored the existing law already by making himself dictator for an unlimited time, but he wanted to go even further. Because he was an aristocrat, Sulla believed that the aristocrats should rule Rome. So he weakened the power of the plebeians and tried to make the senate stronger, as it had been in the past. Soon after he made these changes, however, Sulla retired to private life.

Rome and her citizens had learned a new and bitter lesson. Her law, her senate, and her people were not strong enough to rule the empire. Marius and Sulla had shown that the surest way to rule the Roman Empire was to rule the Roman army, and others would follow their example. The power of the sword was to become more important than the power of the vote. Soon the republic would be ruled by one man—Julius Caesar.

The Time of Julius Caesar

In the year 100 B.C., Julius Caesar was born in Rome. At this time, because Rome was ruler of the world, there were many ships carrying gold from different parts of the empire to Rome. Pirates seemed to be everywhere in the Mediterranean Sea. They sailed up and down, lying in wait to capture and rob these ships laden with gold.

When Caesar grew to be a young man, he went on a journey to Greece, across the Mediterranean Sea. While he was on his way, he was captured by these pirates. They kept Caesar a prisoner and sent a message to Rome saying they would not let him go unless Rome paid a large ransom; that is, unless Rome sent them a great deal of money. Caesar knew that he would be killed if the money was not sent. He knew, too, that he might be killed anyway. But he was not afraid, and told the pirates that if he lived to get back home he would return with a fleet and punish every one of them. When at last the money came, the pirates let Caesar go.

They thought Caesar would not dare to do what he said. They thought he was just "talking big." At any rate, they did not believe he would be able to catch them even if he *did* try. Caesar, however, kept his word. He came after them as he said he would do, and took them prisoners. Then he had them all put to death on the cross, which was the Roman way of punishing thieves.

In 59 B.C. a general named Pompey, a wealthy man named Crassus, and Julius Caesar formed a ruling group called the First Triumvirate. (Triumvirate means three men.) Each was a consul and each was in charge of part of the army and part of the empire. Each had different goals. Pompey wanted to have the Roman people accept some treaties, or agreements, he had made with rulers in the East; Crassus wanted to become richer; and Julius Caesar wanted to conquer and govern Gaul.

The far-off places of the Roman Empire were always fighting against Rome to try to get out from under her rule. Rome had to keep them in order by using force—the force of a general with an army. Caesar was given an army and sent to fight two of these far-off places—Britain (England), and the country north of Spain, which was then known as Gaul. Caesar's army fought well and managed to conquer all of Gaul, even though the Gauls fought very bravely.

He then wrote a history of his battles. The history was written in Latin, which was Caesar's language. This book,

Historical Pictures Service, Chicago

Julius Caesar

called *Caesar's Commentaries on the Gallic War*, is usually one of the first books read by students of the Latin language.

In 55 B.C. Caesar took his army across the Mediterranean Sea, through the English Channel to the island of Britain. He conquered Britain, but went back again the following year to do a more thorough job. He was becoming very famous for the way he conquered and ruled over the western part of the Roman Empire. Besides this, he was very popular with his soldiers.

While Caesar had been fighting in the West, Pompey had been fighting successfully in the eastern part of the Roman Empire. But Pompey was becoming very jealous of Caesar's power and popularity. Crassus had been killed in a war and Pompey felt that if only he could get rid of Caesar, the Roman Empire would be his. So while Caesar was away with his army, Pompey went to the Roman senate and persuaded the senators to order Caesar to give up the command of his army and return to Rome.

Historical Pictures Service, Chicago

Head of Pompey

When Caesar received this order, he thought over the matter for some time. Then at last he made up his mind that he would return to Rome, but he would not give up his command. Instead, he decided that he and his army would take command of Rome.

There was a little stream called the Rubicon which separated Rome from the part of the country that Caesar ruled. Roman law forbade any general to cross this stream with an army ready to fight. This law was made for a good reason. The Romans were afraid that if a general with an army got too close to Rome, he might make himself king.

Caesar decided not to obey the senate. In 49 B.C., he and his army crossed the Rubicon and marched on to Rome. People now say that a person "crosses the Rubicon" when he takes any step that makes it impossible for him to turn back—when he starts something difficult or dangerous that he must finish.

When Pompey heard that Caesar was coming, he fled to Greece. In a few days, Caesar had made himself dictator not only of Rome, but of all Italy. Caesar then went after Pompey in Greece. Caesar defeated Pompey at Pharsalus in 48 B.C.

Now that Pompey was out of the way, Caesar was the chief ruler of the whole of the Roman Empire. Pompey fled to Egypt, and when Caesar went there to find him, he

Alinari-Art Reference Bureau

Statue of Cleopatra. Palazzo Ducale, Venice.

learned that Pompey had been killed. This was the end of the First Triumvirate.

Egypt did not yet belong to Rome. Caesar went there next and conquered that country. In Egypt there was a beautiful queen named Cleopatra. Cleopatra was so charming that she seemed able to make everyone fall in love with her. Cleopatra flirted with Caesar so much that he nearly forgot everything else except his love for her. And even though he had conquered her country, he made Cleopatra queen of Egypt! She still had to obey Rome, however.

Historical Pictures Service, Chicago

Just at this time, some people in Syria and Asia Minor started a war to get rid of the rule of Rome. Caesar left Egypt and traveled rapidly to where the enemy was. He conquered the troublesome people and then sent back the news of his victory to Rome. There were only three words in the message. The messenger could have carried three thousand words as easily as three words, but Caesar wrote only "*Veni, vidi, vici,*" which in Latin means, "I came, I saw, I conquered."

When Caesar returned to Rome in 45 B.C., he was head of the whole Roman Empire. But he wasn't called king, for you remember there had been no kings since 509 B.C., when Tarquin was driven out. The Romans made Caesar dictator for life, even though they had always worked very hard to be sure that one man would never become absolute ruler of Rome.

The senate that was begun in 500 B.C. to represent the people and make laws was no longer important in ruling Rome. Rome now had a one-man rule, not a republic. Julius Caesar was dictator for life, and held the office of a consul, among others. He really had all the power. A few people who thought Caesar had too much power decided on a plot to stop his rule. They were afraid that he would try to become king.

One of the people who joined the plot was Brutus, the man who had been Caesar's best friend. Even though Brutus was Caesar's friend, he believed that the republic was more important than friendship.

On March 15, called the Ides of March, in the year 44 B.C., Caesar was supposed to visit the Roman senate. The men who were taking part in the plot lay in wait for him. Just as Caesar arrived and was about to enter the senate, the plotters crowded around him, and one after another they stabbed him.

Caesar, taken by surprise, tried to defend himself; but all he had was his stylus, which was a kind of pen he used for writing. When Caesar saw Brutus—his best friend—strike at him he cried, "Et tu, Brute!" Which means, "You, too, Brutus!" Then he fell to the floor—dead.

---

left: The death of Caesar on the Ides of March

Augustus Caesar Takes Over

A man who is famous sometimes has a town or a street named after him. But just suppose a month, one of the twelve months of the year, was given your name! Millions and millions of people would then write and speak your name forever!

I'm going to tell you about a man who not only had a month named after him but who was made a god!

After Caesar was killed, three men ruled the Roman Empire. They formed the Second Triumvirate. You remember the First Trimvirate had been formed by Pompey, Crassus, and Caesar. One of the three men in the Second Triumvirate was Antony, who had been one of Caesar's friends. The second was Caesar's adopted son, who was named Octavian. The name of the third was Lepidus, who didn't last long, for Antony and Octavian soon got rid of him. They no sooner had forced him out, however, when each began to plot to get rid of the other.

Antony's share of the empire was in the East. Antony went to live in the capital of this part—Alexandria, Egypt.

In Egypt Antony met and fell in love with Cleopatra, just as Caesar had done before him. And, although he already had a wife—Octavian's sister—he finally married Cleopatra.

At this time, Octavian was in Italy, which was his share of the empire. He didn't like the way things were going and so made war on Antony and Cleopatra. Octavian's army defeated Antony's forces in the battle of Actium on the west coast of Greece in 31 B.C. Soon after Antony committed suicide—killed himself—to avoid being taken to Rome as a prisoner.

Cleopatra flirted with Octavian just as she had with Julius Caesar and Antony. She hoped he would fall in love with her also and save her throne.

But it was no use. Octavian was a different kind of man. Cleopatra saw that it was no use trying her tricks on him. Then she heard that she was going to be taken back to Rome and paraded through the streets, as the Romans did with other prisoners taken in battle. She could not stand

---

opposite: Cleopatra at the Battle of Actium

Historical Pictures Service, Chicago

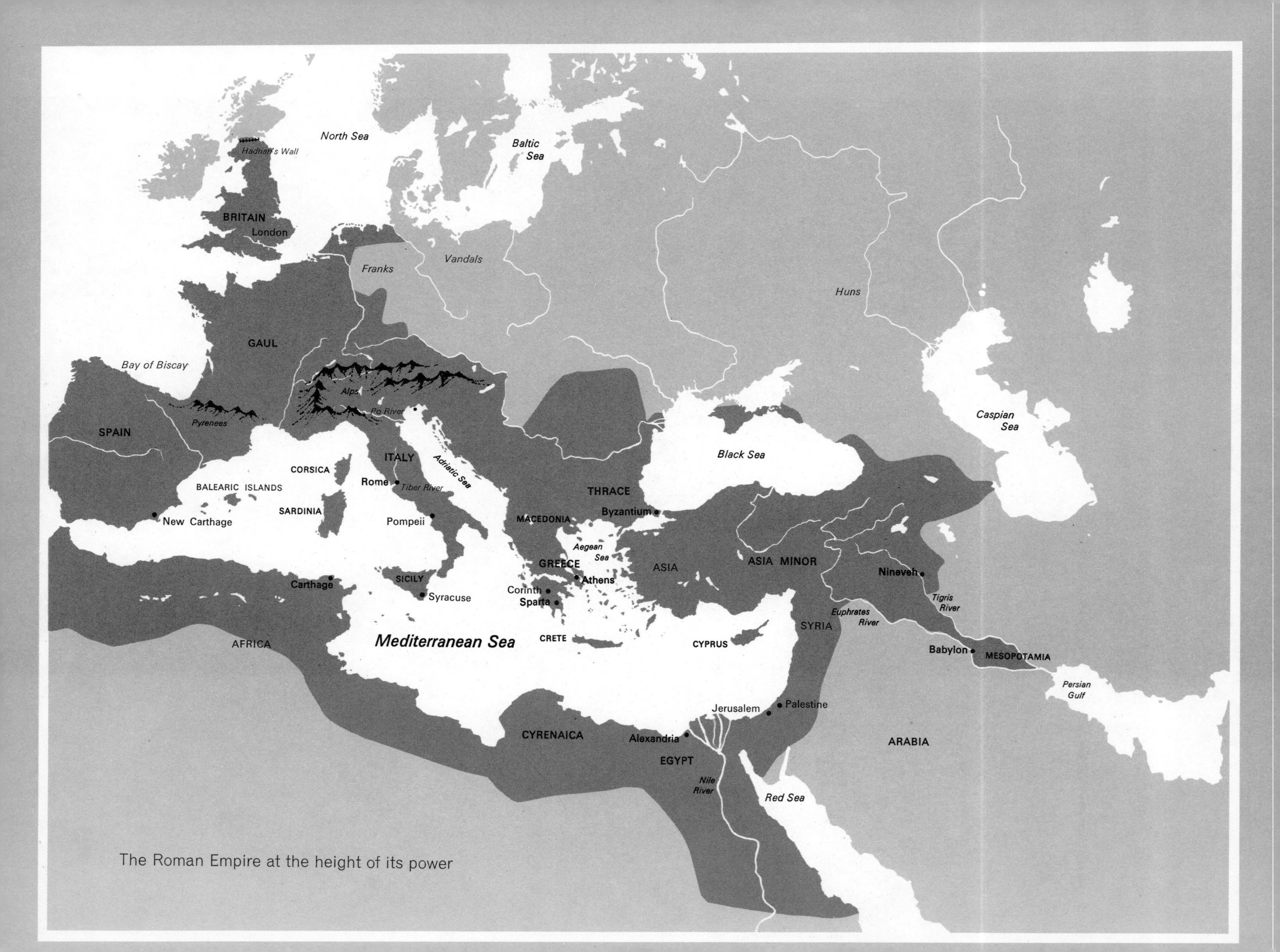

The Roman Empire at the height of its power

such a shame as that, and made up her mind she would not be taken back to Rome. Cleopatra found a poisonous snake called an asp, and let it bite her until she died of the poison.

Octavian made Egypt a Roman province. He now ruled East and West—all the Mediterranean was ruled by one man. In 27 B.C., when Octavian returned to Rome, the people hailed him as their hero. He was given the title *Augustus* by the senate. "Augustus" means "exalted or sacred" in Latin. Rome had seen the last of her kings in 509 B.C., but from now on she had emperors. Emperors had greater power than kings, for they ruled over many countries.

Alinari-Art Reference Bureau

Portrait bust of Augustus.
Museo Nazionale, Naples.

Octavian, now called Augustus, was only thirty-six years old when he became sole master of the Roman world. Rome was the great capital of this vast empire.

Augustus set to work to make Rome a beautiful city. He tore down many of the old buildings made of brick and put up in their place a remarkable number of new and handsome buildings of marble. And so Augustus always bragged that he had "found Rome brick and left it marble."

One of the finest buildings in Rome, the Pantheon, was built. Pantheon means the temple of all the gods. Do not confuse the Pantheon in Rome and the Parthenon in Athens, for the two buildings are quite different. Though the names look something alike, they mean quite different things. "Parthenon" is another name for the goddess Athena. "Pantheon" is from the two words "Pan theon," which means "all gods."

The Pantheon has a dome built of concrete. This dome is shaped like a bowl turned upside down, and in the top of the dome is a round opening called an eye. Though this eye is uncovered, the height is so great above the floor that it is said that rain coming through the eye does not wet the floor beneath, but evaporates before reaching it.

So magnificent did the city become with all these wonderful buildings, and so permanently did it seem to be built, that Rome was known as the "Eternal City"—the city that would last forever. It is still known by this name.

There was a public square in Rome called the Forum. Here markets were held and the people came together for many reasons. Around the Forum were erected temples to

---

left: The Roman Empire at the height of its power

DOMINVM IN SANCTIS EIVS
LAVS EIVS IN

the gods, courthouses, and other public buildings. These courthouses were something like the temples that the Greeks built, only the columns were put on the inside of the building instead of on the outside.

Triumphal arches also were erected to celebrate great victories. When a conquering hero returned from the war, he and his army passed through a specially built arch in a triumphal parade.

We have mentioned the amphitheater in Rome called the Circus Maximus; it is supposed to have held two hundred thousand people—more people than any structure ever built. It was at last torn down to make room for other buildings.

Another Roman amphitheater was the Colosseum, in which were held gladiator fights. This was not built, however, until some time after Augustus had died.

The Colosseum is still standing, and, though it is in ruins, you can sit in the same seats where the old Roman emperors did, see the dens where the wild animals were kept, the doors where they were let into the arena, and even bloody marks that are said to be the stains made by the slain men and beasts.

So many famous writers lived during the rule of Augustus—31 B.C. to 14 A.D.—that this period has been called the Augustan Age. Two of the best-known Latin poets, whose poetry every Latin student now reads after he has finished *Caesar's Commentaries*, lived at this time. These poets were Vergil and Horace. Vergil wrote the "Aeneid," a long poem called an epic poem, which told of the travels of Aeneas, the Trojan. Aeneas finally settled in Italy, and was supposed to have been the great-great-great-grandfather of Romulus and Remus, who legend says founded Rome. Horace wrote many short poems called odes. They were love songs of shepherds and shepherdesses and songs of the farm and country life.

When Augustus Caesar died at the age of seventy-five, he was considered a god because he had done so much for Rome. Temples were built in which the people worshipped him. The month of August is named after him.

---

opposite: The Roman Pantheon

Historical Pictures Service, Chicago

International Visual Aids Center, Belgium

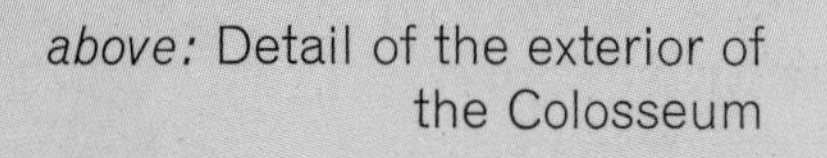

above: Detail of the exterior of the Colosseum

---

right, top to bottom:

A reconstruction of the Roman Forum showing the Via Appia

Interior view of the Colosseum

The Roman Colosseum

Historical Pictures Service, Chicago

International Visual Aids Center, Belgium

International Visual Aids Center, Belgium

The Beginning of Christianity

During the time of Augustas Caesar there lived another very important man. Jesus Christ was from Judea, a region in Palestine that was part of Augustus' eastern empire. People from Judea were called Jews.

Jesus was the son of a carpenter, and as a boy and young man led a very simple and quiet life working in his father's shop. When he was more than thirty years old, he began teaching the people what is called today the Christian religion.

The poorer Jews listened to Christ and believed what he taught them because they thought he was going to set them free from the rule of the Romans, which they hated. The Jewish chief priests, however, were afraid of what Christ taught because so many people listened to him and believed in what he said. So they plotted to have him put to death.

The Jews could not have Christ put to death without the permission of the Roman ruler of that part of the empire where Christ lived. This ruler was named Pilate. They went to Pilate and told him that Christ was trying to make himself king. Christ meant, of course, that he was a heavenly ruler and not an earthly king, but the Jews knew that Pilate would not care at all what religion Christ taught. There were all sorts of religions in the Roman Empire—some that taught belief in idols; some that taught belief in the sun, moon, or stars; and many others. One more new religion would make little difference to the Romans, and Christ would not be put to death simply for teaching another. But the Jewish priests knew that if they could make Pilate believe that Christ was trying to make himself a king, Pilate would have him crucified—that is, put to death on a cross—which was the way the Romans punished criminals.

Pilate did not believe much in what the Jewish priests said against Christ, but it was a small matter to him one way or the other, and he wanted to please them. So Pilate agreed to have Christ crucified, and this was done. Though

Christ lived for only thirty-three years, his teachings created one of the great religions in the world—Christianity.

Christ had chosen twelve of his fellow Jews to teach what he told them about the Christian religion. These twelve men were called apostles. After Christ's death, the apostles went through the land teaching the people what Christ had taught them. Those who believed in and followed his teachings were called disciples of Christ, or Christians. The apostles were teachers; the disciples were pupils.

The Romans thought these disciples of Christ were trying to start a new world empire, and that they were against Rome and the emperor and should be arrested and put in prison. So the Christians usually held their meetings in secret places, sometimes even underground in places called catacombs, so that they would not be found and arrested.

But after awhile the leaders of the Christians became bolder. They came out of their secret places and taught and preached openly, although they knew that sooner or later they would be thrown into prison and perhaps killed.

During the first hundred years after Christ, many Christians were put to death because they were thought to be traitors. Christians who died for their beliefs were called martyrs.

Since in the Christian calendar everything before Christ's birth is called B.C. and everything since his birth is called A.D., you would naturally suppose that the year 0 would have been the date of his birth. But it was not until about five hundred years after his death that people began to measure time from Christ's birth. And when they did begin to do so, a mistake was made. Christ was really born four years before people thought he had been born—that is, in 4 B.C.—but when the mistake was discovered, it was too late to change.

opposite top: Christ preaching by the lake

opposite below: A chamber of a catacomb

Nero and Titus

Every good story usually has a villain to make it interesting. Nero has been considered the prize villain of history. He was a Roman emperor who lived not long after Christ, and many think he was the most cruel and wicked ruler that ever lived.

Nero seemed to take great pleasure in making others suffer. He loved to see men torn to pieces by wild beasts; it amused him greatly.

He was a special enemy of Christians. We think Nero ordered the apostles St. Peter and St. Paul put to death, for they were executed at this same time.

If a man were a Christian, that gave Nero an excuse to torture him horribly. As we have said, Nero was a very cruel man. He had killed his mother, his wife, and his teacher, Seneca. It is even said that he set Rome on fire just for fun. Then he sat in a tower and, while he watched the fire, he played his harp. The saying is that "Nero fiddled while Rome burned." But there were no fiddles at that time, and so we think he probably played a harp. The fire burned day and night for a whole week. It destroyed more than half the city. Nero blamed the Christians for the fire so that the Romans would be even harder on them.

Nero built himself an immense palace and covered as much of it as he could with gold and mother-of-pearl. It was known as Nero's House of Gold. At its front door, he put a bronze statue of himself fifty feet high. Both the House of Gold and the statue were later destroyed. The Colosseum, which was built a few years afterward, got its name from the colossal, or giant, statue of Nero that was once at the door of Nero's palace.

Nero was very conceited. He thought he could write poetry and sing beautifully. Although he did both very badly, he liked to show off, and no one dared to laugh at him. Had anyone made fun of him or even smiled, Nero might have had him put to death instantly.

Even the Roman people who were not Christians feared and hated Nero. So they voted to have him put out of the way. But before they had a chance to do anything, Nero heard what they were planning, and in order to save himself the disgrace of being put to death by his own people he decided to kill himself. He was such a coward, however, that he couldn't quite bring himself to plunge the sword

Historical Pictures Service, Chicago

The death of Nero

into his heart. But as he hesitated, holding the sword to his breast and whimpering, his slave, impatient to finish the job, shoved the blade in.

The Jews in Jerusalem didn't like to have Rome rule over them. They never had. But they were afraid to do much about it. In the year 70 A.D., however, they rebelled; that is, they said they would no longer obey Rome or pay her money. The new emperor Vespasian sent his son, who was named Titus, with an army to put an end to the rebellion and punish the Jews as if they were disobedient children.

Alinari-Art Reference Bureau

Portrait bust of Titus. Villa Albani, Rome.

The Jews crowded into their city of Jerusalem to make a last stand against the Romans. But Titus destroyed that city completely. It is thought that a million Jews perished. Then Titus robbed the great temple of all its valuable ornaments and brought them back to Rome.

To celebrate this victory over Jerusalem an arch was built in the Forum at Rome, and through this arch Titus and his army marched in triumph. On this arch was carved a procession, showing Titus leaving the city of Jerusalem with the captured ornaments. Chief among these ornaments was a golden seven-branched candlestick he had taken from the temple. Today we see many copies of this famous seven-branched candlestick. It is called a menorah. Perhaps you have one in your home.

The city of Jerusalem was rebuilt later, but most of the Jews who were left were scattered through the other countries of the earth.

Pompeii

In Italy there is a volcano named Vesuvius. The word "volcano" comes from the name "Vulcan," the Roman blacksmith god. People imagined that this god's forge was in the heart of a volcano and that it made the smoke and flame and ashes that came forth. From time to time this volcano, Vesuvius, thunders and quakes and erupts, or spouts forth fire and throws up stones and gas and boils over with red-hot melted rock called lava. It is the heat inside of the earth exploding. Yet people build houses and towns nearby and live even on the sides of the volcano. Every once in awhile their homes are destroyed when the volcano quakes or pours forth fire. Yet people go right back and build again in the same place!

During the rule of Titus there was a little town named Pompeii near the base of Vesuvius. Wealthy Romans used to go there to spend the summer. Suddenly, one day in the year 79 A.D., just after Titus had become emperor, Vesuvius began to spout forth fire. The people living in Pompeii rushed for their lives, but they didn't have time to get away. They were smothered with the ashes from the volcano almost before they had time to move and were buried deep in a boiling rain of fire and ashes wherever they happened to be when the eruption took place.

The people and their houses lay buried beneath the ashes for nearly two thousand years, and in the course of time people had nearly forgotten there ever had been such a place as Pompeii. People came back as they had before and built houses over the spot where once there had been a city. Then one day a man was digging a well over the spot where Pompeii had once been. He dug up the hand of a statue. He told others, and they set to work and dug and dug to see what else they could find. Finally these people uncovered the ancient city of Pompeii.

Bob Brunton—Hollis Associates

Alinari-Art Reference Bureau

There are houses that belonged to Romans who went there to spend their vacations. There are shops and temples and palaces and public baths and the theater and the marketplace, or forum. The streets were paved with blocks of lava that had once been melted stone. They still show ruts that were worn into them by the wheels of the chariots the Romans used to drive. Stepping-stones had been placed at some crossings so that in case of heavy rains, when the streets were full of water, one could cross on them from curb to curb. These stepping-stones are still there. The floors of houses were made of bits of colored stone to form pictures, called mosaics. They are still there. In the vestibule of one house, there is in the floor a mosaic picture of a dog. Under it are the Latin words, *Cave Canem.* It means, "Beware of the dog!"

The bones of the people who were caught and buried alive in the ashes were found. There were found also bronze ornaments worn by the women, vases that decorated the home, lamps they used to light the houses, pots and pans, and dishes. Beds and chairs were found just as they had been buried. Still more remarkable, cakes were found on the table, a half-eaten loaf of bread, meat ready to be cooked, a kettle on the fire with the ashes still underneath it—beans and peas and one unbroken egg—probably the oldest egg in the world!

opposite top: The ruin of Pompeii as Vesuvius erupts

opposite bottom: The House of the Gladiators, found in the ruins of Pompeii. Even the frescoes on the walls have been well preserved.

Marcus Aurelius and His Son

After Titus came other emperors. Trajan (98-117 A.D.), a brilliant soldier, paid attention to the Roman provinces and protected the northern frontiers with soldiers. Hadrian (117-138 A.D.) built long walls on the frontiers, and appointed honest government officials to collect taxes. Antonius Pius (138-161 A.D.) held the rule that a man was innocent until proven guilty. Because of these emperors the frontiers of the empire were safe and quiet for a long time. The people under Rome had the protection and peace of Roman rule.

During this time there was a society or club whose members tried very hard not to be upset by the evil things that might happen to them, or excited about the good things. They called themselves "Stoics," and they thought that it was wrong to let things bother them—especially those things over which they had no control.

If a Stoic's house burned down, he would not be upset, but accept it as something he could not have prevented.

If someone gave him a great fortune, he would not be exited as most of us would be, but would accept it calmly.

If he were told by the doctor that he had only a week to live, he would accept it without being upset.

This society of Stoics had been started in about 300 B.C. by a Greek philosopher named Zeno.

Zeno lived in Athens later than Socrates and Plato, whom we have already mentioned. Zeno said that the only way to be good and the only way to be happy was not to care for pleasure and not to mind pain or suffering but to put up with everything calmly, no matter how unpleasant or disagreeable it might be, and the Stoics believed him. Even today people who bear troubles and pain and hardships without a murmur are called stoics.

One of the most important members of the society was a Roman emperor who ruled from 161 A.D. to 180 A.D. Rome's worst emperor, Nero, had been dead a hundred years when there came to the throne this new emperor, who was just as good as Nero had been bad. This emperor was named Marcus Aurelius. Although he was a good man, Marcus Aurelius did not treat the Christians very well, for he believed they were traitors to the empire.

At this time most of the Romans had very little religion of any sort. They were not Christians, but neither did they put much faith in their own gods, such as Jupiter and Juno. They honored them because they were brought up to honor

Historical Pictures Service, Chicago

The Column of Trajan as it stood in the Roman Forum

Alinari-Art Reference Bureau

Alinari-Art Reference Bureau

Alinari-Art Reference Bureau

above, top to bottom:

Portrait bust of Hadrian. Museo Nazionale, Naples.

Portrait bust of Zeno. Museo Nazionale, Naples.

Portrait bust of Marcus Aurelius. Museo Capitolino, Rome.

them and because they thought if they didn't they might have bad luck. But instead of believing in such gods, people usually believed in the teachings of some wise man or philosopher and obeyed, more or less, the rules made by him. Zeno was one of these philosophers, and the Stoics were the members of this society.

Although Marcus Aurelius was an emperor, he would rather have been a Stoic philosopher or a priest. Although he had to be a soldier and a general, he would rather have been a writer. When he was fighting the barbarian invaders with his army in 167 A.D., he carried his writing materials with him. And every night he went to his tent and wrote down his thoughts. These thoughts he called his *Meditations*. Here is one of the things he wrote:

"When you find you do not want to get up early in the morning, make this short speech to yourself. I am getting up now to do the business of a man. Was I made to do nothing but doze and keep warm under the covers?"

That was written long years ago, yet people read this book by Marcus Aurelius today, either in the Greek in which it was written, or in a translated edition of it.

One of his rules was, "Forgive your enemies," and he seemed almost glad to have enemies to forgive. Indeed he took such a special delight in forgiving his enemies that he went out of his way to do so. Though Marcus Aurelius was not a Christian, he acted more like a Christian than some of the later emperors who were supposed to be Christians.

When Marcus Aurelius died in 180 A.D., the two centuries of Roman peace, called the "Pax Romana" also died. For like many people who are very wise and good themselves, Marcus Aurelius had been unable to bring up his son to be equally good or wise. And unfortunately for poor Rome, Marcus Aurelius named his son as his successor.

Alinari-Art Reference Bureau

Portrait bust of Commodus. Villa Albani, Rome.

Commodus was a vain, weak man. Unlike his father, who believed and practiced the philosophy of Zeno and the Stoics, Commodus joined the society of another philosopher called Epicurus.

Epicurus had lived in Greece about the same time as Zeno. But Epicurus had taught what at first seems almost the opposite of what Zeno taught. Epicurus believed that the highest good man could achieve in life was pleasure of body and of mind. This pleasure could only be achieved when man lived wisely, nobly, and justly.

This doesn't sound like a philosophy Commodus would like does it? Well you are right! By the time of Commodus, the society of the Epicurians in Rome had changed this philosophy to suit themselves. They used it to be an excuse for their wild and selfish lives. Thinking only of themselves, they ate, drank, and made merry—satisfying their desire for pleasure and comfort but ignoring their minds.

Commodus' one thought was pleasure, and the worst kind of pleasure at that. He thought only of giving himself a good time, and nothing of giving his people a good, strong government. Commodus didn't like anyone to oppose him and during the thirteen years he ruled Rome, he poisoned or killed anyone who found fault with or criticized him. Finally his evil life caught up with him and he was killed by his enemies.

The Fall of Rome

During the rule of evil Commodus, the Roman government lost control of the empire. Corrupt government officers put tax money into their own pockets. Trade declined and it was almost impossible to move goods from one part of the empire to another because of the many robbers and pirates. Soldiers were not disciplined and often ran wild.

Commodus had been killed before a successor was named, so the empire had no legal ruler. Several men—most of them army generals—fought to get power and there was a civil war. But every time one of these men won and tried to restore order, he was assassinated. For example, between 235 A.D. and 284 A.D., a period of fifty years, Rome had twenty-six different emperors! Only one of these met a natural death—the rest were all killed. These rulers were called "barrack-room" emperors.

Alinari-Art Reference Bureau

Portrait bust of Diocletian. Museo Capitolino, Rome.

But finally a good emperor came to power in Rome. This man also was a barrack-room emperor, but he was very different from all the others. His name was Diocletian (die-uh-klee′shun). He was a good organizer and did something about the bad conditions in the Roman Empire. The empire was too big for one man to run efficiently. Diocletian knew that if it were smaller it would be easier to manage. So he divided the Roman Empire into two parts. In the western part, which included Italy, Gaul, Spain, Britain, and North Africa, Latin was the official language. The capital of the west was Rome. The eastern part included Greece and the land in the Near East, and Greek was the official language. Each part had its own emperor.

Historical Pictures Service, Chicago

Portrait bust of Constantine. Palazzo dei Conservatori, Rome.

Diocletian chose another man to rule the western part of the empire and he himself ruled the eastern part. He drove out the barbarian tribes, stopped the lawlessness, and disciplined the soldier.

Rome became stronger under Diocletian, but things were far from perfect. The rule passed on to others and in 312 A.D., Constantine became emperor. He was the last of Rome's good and famous emperors. At first Constantine was emperor only in the West, but by 324 he became ruler of the whole empire. Two very important things happened during his rule. The first was that Constantine became a Christian and legalized this religion; and the second was that he established a new capital for the whole Roman Empire. Each of these things greatly influenced the history of the world.

There were many people within the Roman Empire who were Christians, but not many of these were rich or important Romans. Because of this, the believers often were persecuted. This happened not so much because the emperors thought the religion was no good, but because they believed that if people didn't at least pretend to worship and pay tribute to the Roman gods, it meant they didn't support or believe in the Roman government.

The story of how Constantine became a Christian is very interesting. In 312 Constantine was fighting one of his rivals for the throne. One night just before a big battle, he dreamed he saw a flaming cross in the sky. Beneath this cross appeared the Latin words, *In hoc signo vinces*, which means "In this sign you shall conquer." Constantine thought this meant that if he carried the Christian cross into battle he would conquer. He thought it would be worthwhile to give the Christian God a trial. So the next day he had his soldiers carry the cross into battle—and he won! Immediately he became a Christian and the next year, as emperor of Rome, he issued the Edict of Milan. This permitted Christianity to exist and even protected the rights of Christians by law. From this time on, all but one of the emperors of Rome were Christians.

The arch of Constantine was built in the Forum of Rome. This arch is a giant monument to Constantine's military victories. If you visit Rome you can still see this magnificent arch.

As we mentioned, Constantine did another very important thing when he was emperor of Rome. Like Diocletian, he preferred to live in the eastern part of the empire. He picked a city called Byzantium for his new capital. The "New Rome" was renamed Constantine's city. In Greek the word for city is "polis." So Constantine's city became "Constantinepolis," and then was shortened to Constantinople.

Before the time of Constantine, there were no weekly holidays. Sunday was no different from any other day.

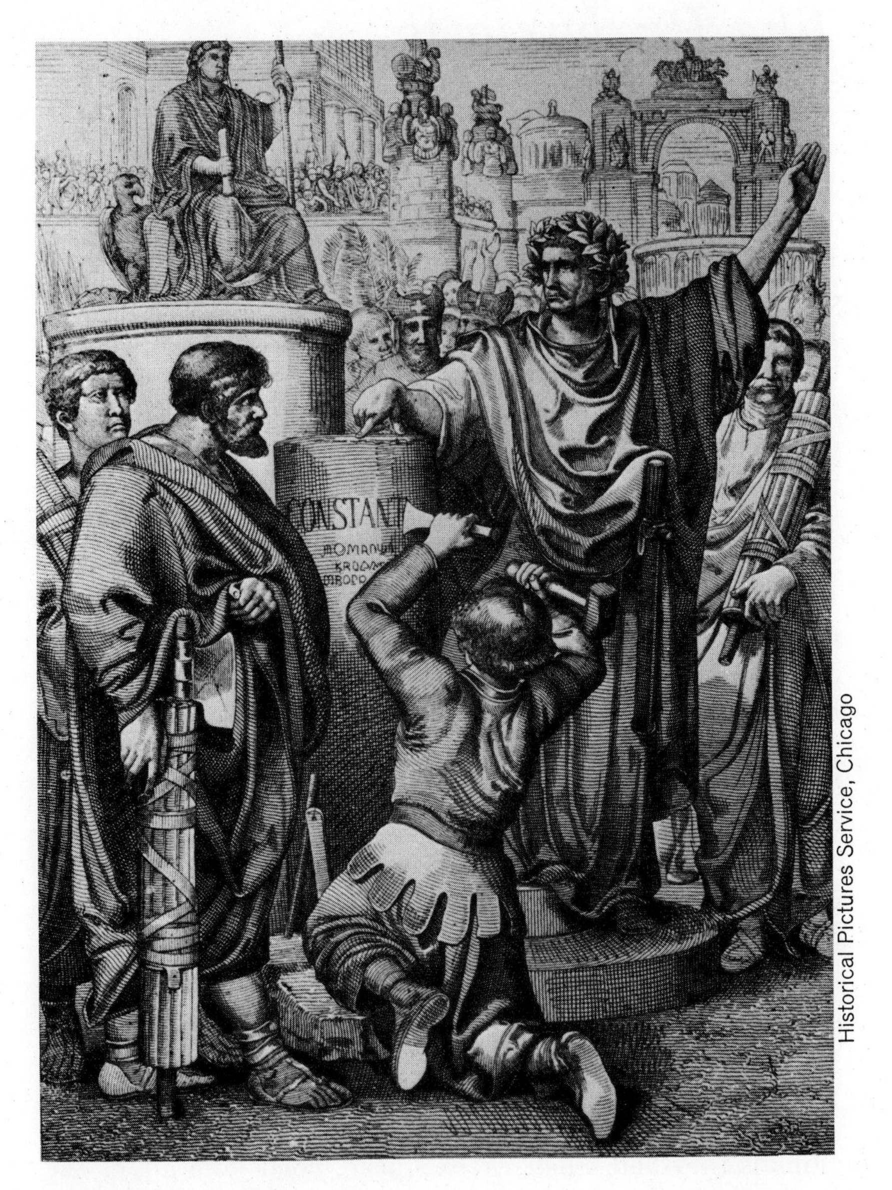

Historical Pictures Service, Chicago

Constantine renames Byzantium

People worked or did just the same things on Sunday as they did on other days. Constantine thought Christians should have one day a week for the worship of God—a "holy day," or "holiday," as we call it—so he made Sunday the Christian day of rest.

Rome and the Roman Empire had had her day as a great political power. She had risen as high as she could and it was her turn to fall. She had become as large as she ever was to be. It was her turn to be conquered.

The Barbarians

For ages there had been a gang of barbarians, or half-civilized people, living on the northern borders of the Roman Empire. Every now and then they tried to cross the border into the Roman lands, and the Romans constantly fought them to keep them back where they belonged. Julius Caesar had fought them. So had Marcus Aurelius, and so had Constantine. These wild and warlike people were called Teutons.

They had light hair and blue eyes; that is, they were what we call blonds. They let their hair grow long as a special mark of their freedom. Most of the Greeks and Romans and other people who lived near the Mediterranean Sea had black hair and dark eyes. They were brunettes.

The Teutons wore skins of animals and rough clothes of linen and wool made by their womenfolk. They lived in huts made of wood, sometimes of branches woven together—like a large basket. Often in winter their home was a hole in the ground. The women raised vegetables and took care of the cows and horses. The men did the hunting and fighting and blacksmithing. Blacksmithing was very important, for the blacksmith made the iron swords and spears with which the Teutons fought, and also the tools and ornaments. That is why the name "Smith" was so honored among them.

When the men went to battle they wore the heads of animals they had killed, an ox's head, horns and all, or the head of a wolf or bear or fox. This was to make themselves look fierce and to frighten the enemy.

About the year 400 A.D. these Teuton or Germanic nations were becoming particularly troublesome to the Romans. They began to push their way down into the northern part of the Roman Empire, and after a few years the Romans could hold them back no longer. Two of these Teuton gangs, or tribes, as they were called, went over into Britain, and the Romans who were living there found it wisest to get out, go back to Rome, and leave the country to the Teutons.

The Teutonic tribes north of Italy were the Goths. They had a leader by the name of Alaric. Alaric and his Goths crossed over the mountains into Italy robbing or destroying everything of value they could lay their hands on. In 410 A.D., they entered Rome and carried away whatever they wanted, and the Romans could not stop them. But the worst was yet to come.

Farther north and to the east of the Teutons was a tribe of people who were still more savage and fierce. They were called Huns. The Huns lived in the far-off forests and wilds, way beyond the Teutons, in a part of the country that no one knew much about.

The Huns were, we think, descended from the Mongolian race. Even the Teutons themselves, fierce fighters though they were, feared the Huns. It was mainly because the Teutons were afraid of the Huns and wanted to get as far away from them as possible that the Teutons went over the borders into the Roman Empire. It was much easier to fight the Romans than it was to fight the Huns.

The Huns seemed more like wild beasts than human beings. Their leader was named Attila, which means, "The Scourge of God." He boasted that nothing ever grew again where his horse had trod. He and his Huns had conquered and laid waste the country from the East almost all the way to Paris. At last the Teutons and Romans in Gaul made a stand against the Huns. In 451 A.D., a great battle was fought at a place not so very far from Paris called Châlons-sur-Marne.

Teutons in war dress

The Teutons fought desperately; they fought madly. After Attila and his Huns had been beaten at Châlons, they left the Teutons alone, and went after the Romans instead. Turning back, the Huns went down into Italy, where no one was able to stop them. They destroyed everything as they moved on. The people of the country didn't even attempt to fight. They thought the Huns were monsters and simply fled before them. So on to Rome the Huns went.

Now at this time there was at Rome a pope named Leo I. Leo, which means "lion," was neither a soldier nor a fighting man, but he and his cardinals and bishops went out from Rome to meet Attila. They were not clad in armor, and none of them carried any weapons with which to fight. The pope and those with him were dressed in gorgeous robes and richly colored garments. It seemed as if they must be slaughtered by Attila and his Huns like lambs before wolves.

But something strange happened when Attila and Pope Leo met; exactly what no one knows. Perhaps Attila was awed by the pomp and splendor of these Christians. At any rate, Attila did not destroy them, nor did he enter Rome but turned about and left Italy.

But no sooner had the dreaded Attila left Rome when the Vandals in Africa saw their chance to attack Rome. And so in 455 the Vandals crossed over from Africa and sailed up the Tiber River to Rome. This time the city had absolutely no defense. The Vandals captured the city without any difficulty. For fourteen days they ransacked Rome taking everything they wanted. And setting sail for Carthage, the Vandals carried away the treasures of Rome.

Poor old Rome! She was at last beaten—beaten for good! She had been the champion for a great many years. But now all her strength was gone. She was old and weak and no longer able to defend herself effectively against these gangs of barbarian tribes. Her empire in the West was falling apart. In fact many of the areas were really being ruled not by the emperor but by barbarian kings. Rome's last emperor was named Romulus Augustulus, the same name of the first king, Romulus, with the addition of Augustulus which means the little Augustus. But in spite of his high-sounding name, Romulus Augustulus could do nothing against the barbarians.

History marks the year that Rome ended as 476 A.D. To say Rome fell is actually misleading. Rather we should say Rome disintegrated from the inside out. Her weak government, undisciplined army, lack of food to feed her people, the poverty caused by the heavy taxes placed on her citizens and the decline of trade and manufacturing left just a shell. A shell that the barbarians could just push aside. This is in fact what happened in the year 476.

A German general named Odoacer (Ode'uh-way-sir), came to Rome and declared himself king. He kicked out the last of the western emperors, Romulus Augustulus, and took control of Italy.

The western half of the empire, of which Rome had been the capital, broke up into little pieces and the pieces were ruled over from then on by various Teutonic leaders. People call this period the end of Ancient History. In the next thousand years, only the eastern part of the Roman Empire, of which Constantinople was the capital, survived. All the rest of the old Roman Empire was completely changed, and new rulers, governments, and ways of living were introduced.

Bob Brunton—Hollis Associates

Attila and his Huns

below: The Huns attacking

Historical Pictures Service, Chicago

INDEX: Young People's Story of the Ancient World, 500 B.C.—500 A.D.

Type *Century Expanded*
Typesetter *American Typesetting Corporation*
Printer *The Regensteiner Corporation*

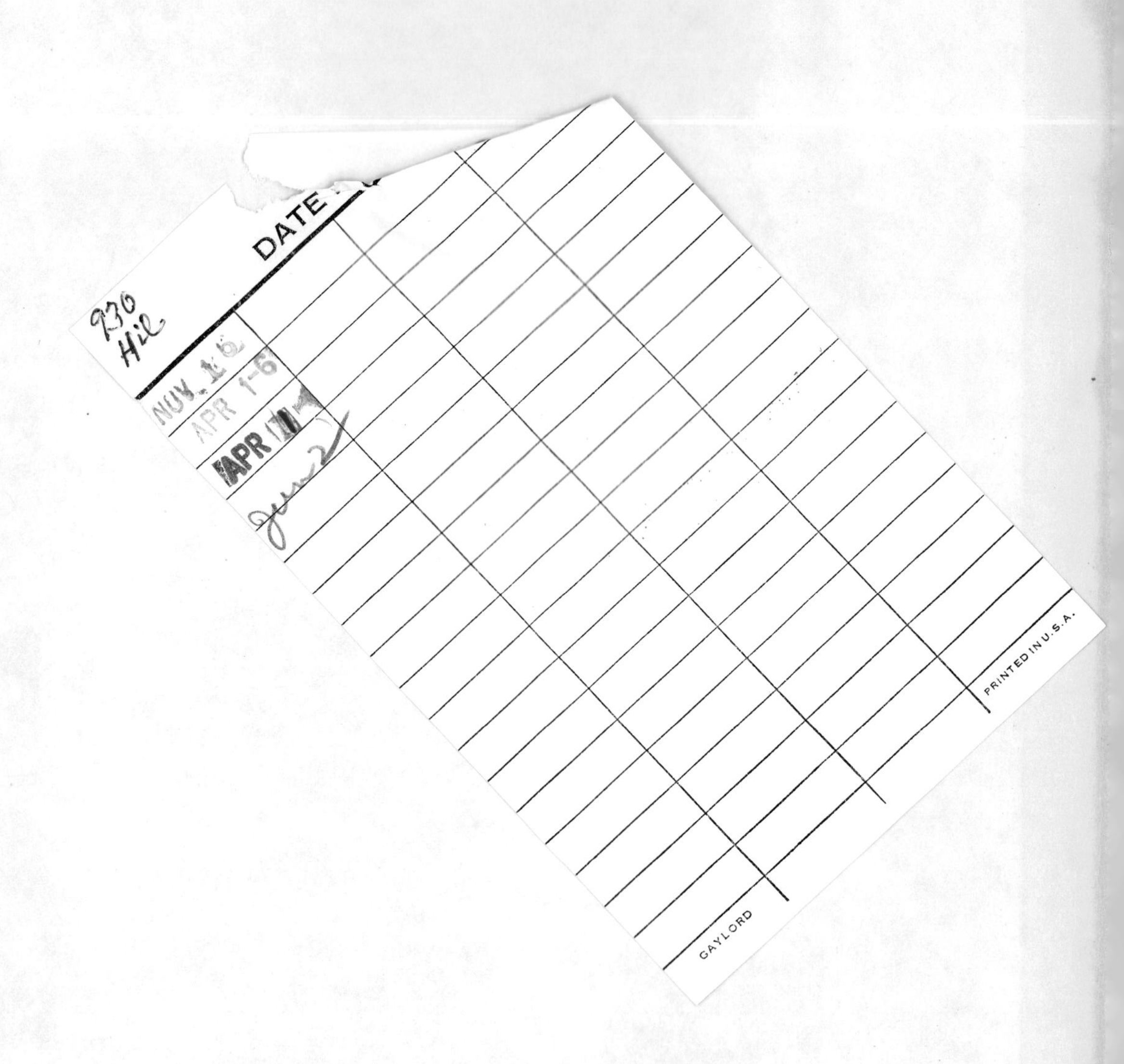

DATE DUE
GAYLORD
PRINTED IN U.S.A.